...Y BLESSING, O Lord, on this book, on ...er, and on all thy people, that with clean ...nd diligent understanding, we may indeed ...In the glory of thy Incarnate Word, full of grace ...d truth.

THE DIVINE WISDOM is at hand; let us attend!

After the Gospel, a sermon usually follows. The preacher's task is to open the readings so that we see ourselves and our world in them, redeemed and made new.

On Sundays and major feast days, the Nicene Creed follows the sermon (or Gospel, if there was no sermon). The creed sums up the Church's faith, and repeating it, we affirm our continuity with those who have followed and believed in Jesus, and our ...nds this faith on to those who will come ...

after us. During the creed, it is common to make a reverence at the words announcing the great mystery of the Incarnation—"he came down from heaven and was incarnate by the... and was made man." Some bow the head at the name of the Incarnation. At the name of Jesus, as this gesture is a remembrance of our baptism. At the name of Jesus, to bow at the name of Jesus, with the Father and Son is worshiped and glorified." At the end of the creed, make the sign of the cross as a remembrance of our baptism.

The intercessions follow, and they sum up the priestly work of the Church and our care for the needs of the world around us. We pray for those we hold dearest—and for the needs of those we may not know, but with whom we share this earth, the frailty and promise of human nature and God's providential care. Silently or aloud, join your prayers with those of others and offer the particular intercessions that are on your heart.

Like the Gospel, the intercessions are particularly associated with the ministry of deacons—who are to interpret the needs of the world to the Church and the Church to the world. In the absence of a deacon, a lay person may lead the prayers of the people. The Prayer Book spells out clearly that intercession is to be offered for "the Universal Church, its members...

TEATIME
DISCIPLESHIP

SALLY CLARKSON

HARVEST HOUSE PUBLISHERS
EUGENE, OREGON

To Clay, for working over 40 years to dream of bringing light to our world with me, over ten thousand cups of tea together.

To our four wonderful children, who have been tea companions over thousands of hours of soul-shaping, reading, meals, and discussion.

To Phyllis, for sharing with me the profound importance of teatime discipleship by extending hospitality to me countless times when I needed personal care and friendship.

To Gwennie, for building that rhythm into our lives in Vienna—even if it was coffee sometimes.

To my myriad wonderful friends who have entered into worlds of love and friendship over cups together through the years.

CONTENTS

AN INVITATION

Lighting a candle on a tiny table near my front living room window looking out on the snow-covered ground, I eagerly anticipate the arrival of my dear friend. I've picked the most pleasant view to the outside aspen trees and the tall pines, so our souls will feast on beauty as we talk.

A small crystal bowl is filled with salted, roasted buttered pecans. A matching bowl of fresh blueberries sits next to it. Dark chocolates wrapped in silver paper—her favorites—are waiting in a small pedestal dish I recovered from a secondhand store. My old Austrian teapot is filled to the brim with strong Yorkshire Gold tea, a favorite of my guest...and mine!

I have already pondered the questions I will ask to make our time purposeful because I know it will pass too fast. I will look into her eyes and even notice the wrinkles around them, the demeanor of her countenance, because I want to see into her heart. How has life treated her during these past months? Is there a furrow in her brow? What challenges has she encountered? What books has she been reading? And I will take her hand in mine and tell her how very glad I am to be with her and how much I love her. I will ask, "How can I pray for you today?"

I can't even begin to count how many close friends I have made over a simple meal or a cup of tea (or coffee, if you must!). There is something about stealing time away from the "busy" of life and sipping something wonderful, smooth, and warm while sitting in an environment where secrets can be shared, silly moments discussed, sympathy poured out, comfort given, and dreams become real in the speaking. I think of strong coffees in Vienna with new friends long ago, of daily pauses at three o'clock with friends in Oxford, both of which gave me a love for afternoon teatimes. *Civilizing of the heart and soul*, I have called it. Of Saturday morning omelets and the cheesy egg quesadillas that knit my heart to my sweet children. Of the foundational traditions of teatimes on my front porch or with warm chocolate chip cookies on my back porch.

All of this is teatime discipleship. When the atmosphere has been created and the table has been laid with intentionality and care, we are drawn together to learn, encourage, and strengthen

From years of being intentional with one another, we have a heritage of heart sharing that has sustained both of us.

one another, welcoming one another into the deep things of God, the multifaceted dimensions of His love expressed.

My teatime discipleship journey began in earnest 45 years ago in communist Poland. In the late 1970s, spiritual gatherings were illegal in countries controlled by the Communist Soviet Union. Yet the women who came to us, mostly university students, were eager to learn, hungry to know that their lives had purpose, that a personal God really existed, saw them, and called them His beloved. They took a risk coming to our home to learn more of the Bible.

Leaders in the Polish underground student movement had invited our ministry into the country to teach the Bible and essential truths about living a flourishing Christian life. I was single and moved there with a friend under the guise of being university students. Many weeks, 35 women from cities all over Poland crowded into our modest living room. An ocean of interesting faces—all chattering, laughing, delighting in the company of kindred spirits. They sat on the floor, on wobbly and various chairs, squishing together on two worn couches, squeezing into every nook and cranny. With notebooks in hand and open, our friends gathered for a Bible lesson they would take back to share with groups of women in their cities.

Using every possible cup, mug, and glass, we filled our teapots

with steaming hot water and herbate—the Polish word for tea. Herbate was drunk from glass cups with metal handles to keep our hands from burning. We scooped spoonfuls of sugar into this brew, as was their custom—no milk for them! Piles of buttered bread with jam were passed around, occasionally accompanied by thick slices of pungent cheese. This comprised the feast that made our gathering a celebration.

Here I would learn the gift of teatime—speaking together about eternal truths and life-changing messages of God's love and design, shaping the foundations of thought, sharing in friendship. All of this was made possible simply by opening our doors, serving a simple meal, and establishing an environment of welcome. I drew from these experiences of faith, learned simple hospitality, and forged relationships with seeming strangers in all the years of my ministry. Our experience in reaching out to others and seeing the transforming of their lives set me up for a practice of teatime discipleship for the rest of my life.

One of the reasons I wanted to write this book was to rekindle the understanding that women need women, friends with whom to share life, companions through seasons, and spiritual mentors to keep their faith alive. My heart for my own teaching and messages is to help women feel seen, to help them understand that God is present. He cares for the burdens we carry. Yet, I also hoped to inspire you and others to see that sharing our love, faith, and friendship is not frivolous; it is a necessity if we are to stay alive in Christ. Finding accountability and support is essential to all human beings. We long for love, for a place to belong where we are accepted, limitations and all. We breathe only through the oxygen of love and will die spiritually if we do not have relationships where we can feel kindred with others who understand us, who will join hands with us amid the demands of life.

Come to this book as if I've just met you at the door to welcome you into my home. Candles are lit; soft music is playing. I invite you to choose a china teacup from the cupboard and sit beside me to share stories. Inside these pages you'll find some of my own stories and some of the wisdom I've gleaned over decades of following the Lord. You'll find prayers, recipes, Scripture, stories, books, traditions—all sorts of blessings close to my heart that I would offer you if you sat beside me. And you'll find questions I'd like to ask you to get to know you better—questions you might like to contemplate during an encouraging conversation with a friend during your own teatimes.

In Part One, we'll explore together what it means to create a space for others. I'll bring you into my home and invite you to likewise welcome people in your community. In Part Two, we'll see what it means to be a true friend, discovering how God can transform our hearts, habits, and hospitality when He lives within us. In Part Three, we'll discuss ways to share the message that has changed us. You don't need to be a Bible scholar to love others well! And finally, we'll look in Part Four at what it means to be home to one another—to invite one another into fellowship and joy. I hope to pass on a little of what I've learned in hopes that you, too, might be able to share with others the beauty of a life and moments redeemed by celebrating life in Christ.

God called me to disciple others at a young age, and I've never gotten over the habit. May you, too, discover the joy of sitting at the Master's feet and gathering others around you to hear and celebrate this love and beauty!

~ A BLESSING ~

DEAREST HEAVENLY FATHER,

I love these precious women who are joining me here—and I know You love them more. I pray You will speak compassion, gentleness, and grace through the truth written here. Let Your love, Your compassion, fill their hearts. Give them a feeling of Your deep sympathy, a richness of Your joy, an imagination of the light You want to show through them. From this well of Your goodness, open the doors for them to extend Your generous self and words to those who long to know this beauty of being Your precious child.

Give them eyes to see those around them from the cries of their hearts, not just from their outward selves. Send them into conversations and friendships that bring life and healing. Lord, I know that in heaven we will share together the amazing stories of how You used our lives to bring light and restoration to those You brought our way. Bless and bless and bless these precious ones to flourish and to find Your companionship in their lives a living reality. I come to You in the precious name of Jesus.

AMEN.

PART ONE

WELCOME IN

Our home and table can be a sanctuary for life, a holding place for all our ideals, an atmosphere of love, and an energy that engages dreams and inspiration. The profound work of a woman is to bring civility and order out of chaos, to bring beauty, intelligence, and excellence to her community, and to subdue her kingdom of home into a life-giving haven.

A SPACE TO SHARE

There are few hours in life more agreeable than the hour dedicated to the ceremony known as afternoon tea.

HENRY JAMES, *The Portrait of a Lady*

Our life's greatest work is giving ourselves over to the elegance of God's design, the artistry of His hand, and the loveliness of His presence. And so we can let our lives and homes reflect our will to celebrate each day as He has given it to us.

Treasure seeking is a cherished hobby of mine. To me, it is a sort of art form for bringing fun, beauty, and creative thought to my tables for teatimes.

One Saturday afternoon in Oxford found me strolling along the cobbled streets for an irresistible pastry to grace our tea table the next day. I was headed for a neighborhood shop that specializes in buttery, sugary, melt-in-your-mouth cinnamon buns. Just before I reached the bakery, a secondhand shop across the street called me to peek inside. I glanced around at the artifacts piled near the window and had almost concluded that nothing in the shop would entice me when I spotted a small, intricately woven rattan child's chair in the back corner.

What a find! I could just picture my granddaughter feeling proud of having her own grown-up chair to sit in as we

sipped tea together. I wrestled it into my grasp to walk a half-mile home as a surprise for her. When she first received "Lily's throne," her tiny feet dangled above the floor. Yet now, at age four, it is a perfect fit.

When I visit Lily's home, two hours away in another part of England, I tell her, "Let's let Mama sleep just a bit more. You and I will be friends and talk and tell stories and have a cup of tea every morning. You in your chair and I in mine." And so we do.

We have chattered together and giggled, and she has broken out in wild ballet dancing around the room as we sipped. Now every time I go to visit, she says, "I can't wait till we can be friends again and have our tea together."

As artists in our homes, we paint the canvas of our life stories with the colors we most love, the art and photographs and framed quotations we set in the center to discuss, the way we place furniture to create community, and the ways our tables are decorated to say, "Come here and feast and rest a while. Good food, conversation, and friendship are awaiting you. I have prepared a place for us. You are special and I love spending time with you." I love to love my people well; it brings me much pleasure to plan for ways to delight them, to bring unique touches into my environment that I know will especially please them, cultivating the ambience that will set the stage.

Almost all the time, I leave my tables set to be ready in case anyone comes at any time, so that they can feel I had prepared for them—that I am so very glad they had come.

Music is almost always heard humming through the rooms of my home at any time of day someone might arrive. I pick acoustic instrumental music for the backdrop of conversational evenings, upbeat contemporary artists for cooking together and preparing the feast while in the kitchen, Celtic in the winter evenings as the candles are lit and soup and warm homemade bread is piled in baskets with pungent cheese to accompany pots of steaming tea.

As Easter approaches, rabbits have been seen to hop onto my table. In spring and summer, various figurines of birds peek out of many corners of the place settings. Toy knights or superheroes occasionally grace the settings to delight our boy crowd. Around Christmas, a tiny mouse or angel comes to delight. Multicolored and varied sized vases have been purchased over years at garage sales to hold something natural from the out-doors. Flowers of every sort and color, pine boughs tucked into vases, and wildflowers fresh from the fields surrounding us fill the different corners of our rooms.

The wise woman builds her house.
PROVERBS 14:1

Many years ago, I wanted to provide cozy, two-person high teas (more of a meal and pot full of tea). These were accompanied by small finger sandwiches, a fruit soup, salads, chocolates, and tiny cakes made in muffin tins. I scoured the local antique shops and found a real prize of a piece. It was an old, squeaky-wheeled tea trolley with two sides that folded down when not in use. I could set up this movable treasure between two overstuffed chairs in my den and it became an elegant place setting for a quiet, intimate spot. I have rolled this into bedrooms and onto the front porch, and it has drawn together many a twosome. My children

loved it when I celebrated a special 15-minute mama-tea in their rooms with my little candlelit, treat-laden trolly.

As I grew in imagination as an artist in my home, creating *place* became a satisfying work of my life. I owned the fact that I shaped my life according to my personality and preferences. My desire for delight and whimsy was embodied in how I created the moments for intimacy and friendship, and I realized that I was quite free to do it "my way." There is no one sort of teatime or decor or place where planned mentoring, encouragement sessions must be enacted. All the details are merely the backdrop for the enactment of memories, traditions, love, and legacy. And so, your teatimes will become a unique reflection of *you*—your stories, your delights, and your joys!

Describe a time when you've received extraordinary hospitality. What preparations, words, and actions from your host made you feel welcome?

How can you leave everyone who enters your space with the fragrance, intelligence, and beauty of Christ? What tangible steps can you take to prepare your space for both hospitality and discipleship? How will the presence of Christ be experienced in your home?

RHYTHMS OF PEACE

*When tea becomes ritual, it takes its place at the heart of
our ability to see greatness in small things. Where is beauty
to be found? In great things that, like everything else, are
doomed to die, or in small things that aspire to nothing, yet
know how to set a jewel of infinity in a single moment?*

MURIEL BARBERY, *The Elegance of the Hedgehog*

For as long as I could remember, in the dim, early morning light, I had prepared for the external pressures of the day and entered into a time just for me. In this place, I had poured out lament to God, sought refuge from the storms of life, and found wisdom for my days. I refueled my mind and heart, preparing myself to go back into the battle of life restored, better able to face the demands of my day. Not a luxury, but a necessity for the many demands of my life through seasons.

One recent morning, weary to my toenails, I forced myself to roll out of bed and enter back into the world of responsibility. International jet lag was in full force, so a combination of exhaustion and the inability to sleep left me hollow.

A six-week trip to five cities in the UK—countless train rides, sleeping in beds not my own, packing and unpacking suitcases—had taxed my body, mind, and spirit. Visiting my daughter for the birth of her second child, a precious little boy, while helping her care for my delightful two-year-old granddaughter had given me deep pleasure as well as physically exhausting days. A short two-day trip to London with a dear friend and visiting two other children—graduate students in Scotland— had made my journey all the fuller...and lengthier.

Easing down the stairs from my bedroom in the direction of the kitchen, my wrinkled pajamas seemed to match my weary mood. But unexpectedly, as I filled the kettle with fresh water and reached into my cupboard, piled high with favorite teacups, peace engulfed me. My anxious thoughts were settled. My old tea-cup seemed to whisper calm and gentleness to the depths of my being. Thousands of mornings spent steeping strong Yorkshire Gold tea, sitting in my comfy couch, lighting candles, and playing my favorite soft music had predisposed me to feeling this comfort and pleasure even before I settled into my familiar routine. Perhaps I was having my own Pavlovian response, conditioned by years of repetition, but truly, I felt unexplainable joy and hopeful anticipation wash over me. This habit is the best and most profound rhythm that shaped my whole destiny, I believe.

Sitting down with a cup of tea, meeting God in my armchair, I am open to His leading. So is it any wonder that on that morning when I approached my cherished old tea cabinet, delightful emotions greeted me? I was home once again after a long journey away. The outer trappings of my teatime ritual—my teapot, candles, and soft music—showed that the sacred meeting place was still waiting for me, welcoming me into the rest and peace and deep joy I had experienced so many times before.

Once the stage is set, I'm ready for time with the Lord. At first, sometimes I just sit and stare into the world around me, centering myself. For me, my quiet time begins with my Bible. Often I read

a short devotional. Sometimes, heartfelt prayers pour out; other times, gratitude abounds. Often, I am distracted—but thousands of days spent meeting with Him, pondering His words, and pouring out my heart have built a haven of closeness and intimacy with Christ, my constant companion. Journaling thoughts and prayers has given me a pathway into His presence. This life-giving personal time prepares me for all that my day will hold.

As I established my teatime devotional habits, I early invited my wee children to join me, to enjoy intimate companionship in my life-giving refuge. Squishing together with me on the couch, sipping my tea, I would share what I was reading, what I had thought. And then I'd kiss them on the head and ask what they thought, engaging them in conversation.

Sometimes, I created personal moments for them. I can still picture my eldest daughter, Sarah, at ten years old, sitting cross-legged beside me on our king-sized bed, sipping a cup of hot tea and savoring the adultness of the moment as we stole away in my bedroom. I knew that as she was moving toward her teen years, she could use a little alone time with me to explore her thoughts, emotions, fears, and needs. This moment led to a years-long tradition that built us into best friends. Our sacred tradition of teatime devotions led to deep spiritual mother-daughter discussions. On other nights we studied the Bible together, exchanged secrets with a whisper, and just giggled a lot, sharing the mundane and yet meaningful moments of our days.

Then, when most other mothers I knew faced an empty nest, I had another precious little one, sweet Joy, when I was 42. So I started our tradition all over again, storing up hundreds of hours of shared teatime, friendship, and discipleship—in my bedroom away from the others for stolen moments. Of course, I widened my tradition to include my two boys, and the invested hours knit my heart to theirs. Tolkien and Lewis had paved the way for those tea-times. Along the way, I began to invite my very best friends into these magical moments to share the soul-deep insights of our own lives together.

Over time, my teatime habit became a foundation of my days. Taking the time, making the space in the middle of a busy day for a second teatime moment, I would focus on a real live person and share friendship over a cuppa as a way of connecting with neighbors, other women, my children, my husband—and even with my swirling, hurried self. A cup of tea was no longer only for my benefit; it became an opportunity to invest in those around me. I want to pass on this glorious, sacred, simple tradition to you, so that you, too, can find the special retreat waiting for you to enjoy.

If ministering to others over a cup of tea sounds intimidating to you, first imagine yourself as a follower of Jesus, coming in from a hot day and a dusty road. Imagine Jesus, kneeling down, lovingly touching and firmly wiping the feet of His beloved friends—amid noise, eating, laughing, and living. Imagine Him reaching His

friends' hearts, souls, and minds with truths that would comfort, wisdom that would last: the depth of the call of the kingdom. Ministry, for Jesus, meant embracing the reality of daily life—eating and drinking and conversing.

Jesus didn't just talk about having a ministry from a broad, tall pulpit with a resounding microphone, disappearing between sermons. He lived a deeply personal life, bowing His own knee to meet the needs and desires of those He loved. He taught compassion, and then He demonstrated it by healing the sick, touching people with leprosy, sharing meals with those society had rejected, giving the grace of forgiveness to those who felt shame, holding and caressing children, and feeding those who were hungry.

We, too, can be recipients of that compassion, of the Christ who meets us in the dirt and washes us with living water. And we can pass along that compassion to those we are privileged to serve.

If you're a woman who's too hard

on herself, let me affirm you and the work you do.

You are making a difference in this world. Your work is

eternal. Don't give up what you are doing—ever, ever, ever.

But take a break. You are exactly the one to live your story

well. Find your anchor. Create space in your life where

you can have a few minutes alone each day—a time when

no one wants anything, no task is accomplished—just a

few moments to breathe. Make a habit of spending time in

God's Word daily. Place spiritually uplifting books

near a chair you sit in so that reading even

just a bit of inspiration is easy to do.

TEATIME

To me, teatime is an event, a concerted decision to stop and steep in the moments of time I have taken to prepare my soul, whatever time of day.

My favorite tea—the kind I'll reach for during my morning quiet times and my afternoon cuppa—is Yorkshire Gold. It's a rich black tea, and a good strong cup with milk and sugar that creates an anchor in my day. Perhaps you, too, have a favorite tea—a flavor you'll happily reach for no matter the day, time, or weather. But if you're ready to try something new, there are hundreds of types and flavors from which to choose!

Black Teas

Green Teas

White Teas

Oolong Teas

Herbal Teas

The Perfect Cuppa

Start with fresh water in your kettle. Once it's just at a boil, swirl a little hot water in your teapot and your cups to take off the chill. A cold cup leads to lukewarm tea, after all.

Add a tea bag to your pot for each person, plus one—if it is an average-sized pot. (Or just put a bag in each cup, as I do, to make it delightfully strong.) Sometimes I use a few bags of Yorkshire Gold and add an extra bag of Earl Grey. It gives a little zing of taste to a whole pot. Let the tea steep for a few minutes—don't rush this! This is the perfect moment to nibble a treat or add a splash of milk to your cup. This is a paradigm of life: Take time to let issues of life steep. Wait for the flavor and strength to fill moments with grace.

Once your tea has brewed, pour some into each cup. If you sip tea in the English tradition as I do, it must be a strong brew with milk—not cream—and some sugar to taste. (If you prefer herbal or something milder, a slice of lemon, a spoonful of honey, or maple sugar will do.)

BLACK TEAS

These teas are made with fermented tea leaves and produce a hearty brew that has a higher caffeine content than many other teas. You can drink them plain or with milk and something sweet—as one does with chai. Steep them for five minutes to get the fullest flavor. Try...

English breakfast or *Irish breakfast* to help you greet the morning and get you out the door. These are robust tea blends with complex flavors.

Earl Grey, an aromatic blend of black teas with bergamot oil. These teas are lovely with a dash of lemon.

Assam, an Indian tea with a smooth finish.

Lapsang souchong, called "the king of teas"! This has a rugged, smoky flavor, and historians say it's one of the oldest black teas.

GREEN TEAS

Green tea leaves are steamed just after they're harvested. These are bright, refreshing teas with numerous health benefits. Don't add sweetener, dairy, or lemon to green teas; drink them plain to let the full flavor come through. Steep them for two to three minutes, depending on the variety, in water that's not quite boiling. Try...

Matcha, a cleansing tea with a vegetal taste. Try this with something chocolate to nibble!

Jasmine, a floral tea scented with jasmine flowers. This tea is lovely for a few moments of midmorning peace.

Sencha, a tea with a grassy flavor. If you infuse this briefly in water that's not quite boiling, you'll find it has a smooth, almost sweet taste.

WHITE TEAS

White tea leaves are picked early in the season and left to dry in the sun. These are the least processed of any tea leaves, and they have a clear, delicate flavor. White teas don't have much caffeine, so they're perfect for a late-afternoon pick-me-up. These are best enjoyed without sugar or honey and should be steeped for five to eight minutes. Be sure to use hot water that's not quite boiling, as boiling water can ruin the flavor of white tea. Try...

Silver Needle, which has a pure, floral aroma and a light golden color.

White Peony tea is a little stronger and a little darker than Silver Needle.

OOLONG TEAS

Oolong tea leaves come in a variety of flavors and aromas—from sweet to smoky and everywhere in between! These teas have complex, subtle flavors. If you can, choose loose-leaf varieties, which are higher in quality and more flavorful. Steep these teas anywhere between one and five minutes, depending on your preferences.

HERBAL TEAS

Most herbal teas are free of caffeine—perfect for when you'd like a hot cup just before bed. These aren't made from true tea leaves, but blends of roots, seeds, and fruits of different plants. You'll be able to find many herbal teas available for sale, but you can also try brewing your own by infusing herbs in near-boiling water for a few minutes. Most herbal teas should be steeped for three to five minutes, but they typically don't become bitter if you steep them even longer. Try...

Rooibos, which is a lovely red tea made from the leaves of a South African plant.

Peppermint tea is a simple infusion of dried peppermint leaves. Try this after a large meal; peppermint is a wonder at soothing stomachs (though, oddly, I am allergic to it).

Ginger tea is made from dried and ground ginger root. Try a cup with a squeeze of lemon and a spoonful of honey.

Echinacea tea is a soothing remedy when you're feeling under the weather.

Hibiscus tea has a deep red color that comes from the flower of the same name. This has a bit of a cranberry flavor, and it's refreshing drunk either hot or cold.

Chamomile tea is a blend of dried flowers from the chamomile plant. This has a lovely, gentle flavor that can help you relax in the evening and prepare for sleep.

THE CALLING CARD OF GOD

Never lose an opportunity of seeing anything beautiful. Beauty is God's hand-writing—a way-side sacrament; welcome it in every fair face, every fair sky, every fair flower, and thank Him for it, the fountain of all loveliness, and drink it in, simply and earnestly, with all your eyes; it is a charmed draught, a cup of blessing.

CHARLES KINGSLEY

There is something in God's very nature that must express itself in beauty. Beauty is one of those attributes of God's world that hushes us in quiet admiration. Whether it's a bright rainbow or a luminous sunset, a vibrant red tree frog or a sleek white arctic fox, a proliferation of wildflowers or the natural cathedral of the Redwood forests, creation is evidence of a very colorful master Artist. This is what God does, and as imitators of Christ, we can also cultivate and create this beauty in our own spheres of influence.

Wherever a garden blooms beautifully or a meal draws us to table, someone has invested in planting a seed, tilling the ground, planning the menu, gathering and cooking the food, and preparing the table. Beauty comes about from someone who took the time to craft it, and the crafting adds dimension and pleasure to our lives, even as God did when He created the world in all its splendor.

God is the Author of all creation—including waterfalls, roses, puppy dogs, storms, color, sound, food, and all delights. He is the One who gave us the instinct to giggle and belly laugh; to sway and swirl with the sounds of pulsing music; to delight in the galaxies aglow on a summer night; to touch, kiss, hug, and love; to work and bring out color and beauty from a well-planted garden, a well-written story, a well-set table; to create a meal to delight the palate; to nurse the ill back to health. Our lives should reflect this greatness of God, this *joie de vivre* through the ways we face and celebrate life each day. Beauty is, in fact, the calling card of God. When we intentionally create beautiful places and cultivate splendid spaces, we offer hope in a dismal world, light to the darkness. We are co-creators with God.

A Call to Your Elegance

How do we move from the mundane to the beautiful? We become artists in our home, bringing color and design to our rooms. We are romanticists, touching and caressing and singing love into the hearts of our companions, loved ones, friends. We dance through the music and sing loudly as we wash dishes. We celebrate life each night as we eat and drink together, sharing not just the table but the culture of our family life.

Instead of passing others by, we look deeply into the eyes of these creatures of God. We see inside their hearts and affirm the beauty there and invest words that validate their significance. God's nature expresses itself in beauty. We can participate in this process by cultivating an atmosphere of beauty and calling each other to our elegance.

As women, we have a table, so to speak, of our friends and families. Each has a history and some scars and blemishes. A woman's glory is strongest when she understands her capacity to beautify

the "table" of her community, perhaps redeeming the design she has been given. She can nourish souls and spirits with the rich food of God's Word. She can provide grace and peace as she accepts and wipes up the spills of life. She can celebrate the ordinary days by establishing and commemorating joyful traditions and milestones achieved—however small. She can foster the taste of greatness through the stories and books read and shared. She can establish a spirit of graciousness by welcoming all who come as guests of the true Great Hospitality, where all are served and all are made whole.

In the English language, the words *hospital, hospice,* and *hospitality* all have a common root. The root word implies caring for needs or providing for a guest. When we become hosts, we take responsibility for the care of those under our roofs. Just as a nurse sees to the needs of her patients, a host provides for the comfort and security of all who cross her doorstep. Hosting doesn't have to mean fancy silverware and the nicest teacups. It simply requires a willingness to consider the other more important than oneself, to say: "Tell me your story. I would love to know more about you."

When Jesus lived among us, He recognized people's needs and made a habit of providing for them. He miraculously shared a simple basket of food with 5,000 people. He broke bread and poured wine at Passover. And one morning after the resurrection, Jesus greeted His disciples with a fire, ready to cook the fish they'd just caught. Knowing Jesus, loving Jesus, how could we walk in His spirit and not offer the same provision to our neighbors?

I picture that I can be an instrument through which God can bring life and beauty and redemption to the limitations of my marriage, family, and community. In God's Holy Spirit, I am filled with the life that always brings light to the dark places and redemption to the broken places.

HOME IS...
...the place where chairs are rocked.
...where relationships are
nurtured and prioritized.
...where souls are refreshed.
...where hands are held.
...where you bring hearts together.

CONVERSATION AND CONTEMPLATION

Home is indeed a place of grace—where we can be ourselves, cuddle up to familiarity, count on food we are used to, and expect love that is always and forever unconditional. It is such an honor that God has trusted each of us to be cultivators of beauty within the walls where our loved ones reside.

Still, whether you've spent years in your home or are just starting over, it is easy to feel overwhelmed by work when you think about home. Today, I challenge you to be inspired by all of the amazing, beautiful, lively moments that can and will happen in your home. Write a philosophy statement for the space you cultivate and welcome people into. What words define the home you'd like people to experience?

_____

_____

_____

_____

_____

_____

_____

_____

_____

_____

_____

_____

_____

KINDRED

Oh, the comfort—the inexpressible comfort of feeling safe with a person—having neither to weigh thoughts nor measure words, but pouring them all right out, just as they are, chaff and grain together; certain that a faithful hand will take and sift them, keep what is worth keeping, and then with the breath of kindness blow the rest away.

DINAH CRAIK, *A Life for a Life, Vol. II*

Deep, dark loneliness was a constant companion of my heart for many years. I ached inside for a friend or someone who cared for me—someone who would even notice me. I had known deep friendship, but it seemed that once I became a mother, no one was there—and no one reached out to me. We faithfully attended many groups, meetings, and studies, but we were mainly the ones reaching out. Often, we just didn't seem to fit the mold of other people's expectations.

I remember once when Sarah, my daughter, was washing dishes as a child, she said, "Wouldn't it be nice if someone would invite our whole family over for dinner and we wouldn't have to be the ones who cooked, cleaned, and washed dishes—again?" Even at the age of 12, she wondered at the seeming loneliness of our family as a group. The kids made friends over the years as we moved from place to place, and we always had people we "did stuff" with, but very few kindred spirits came our way.

I knew and felt that I desperately needed a friend—someone to share my joys, burdens, celebrations, and struggles. Ecclesiastes 4:9-10 teaches, "Two are better than one because they have a good return for their labor; for if either of them falls, the one will lift up his companion. But woe to one who falls when there is not another to lift him up!" *Woe to the one who falls.*

That was me, with no one to lift me up. I longed to find a woman who could teach me about marriage, motherhood, and all the rest!

I wrote in my journal what kind of friend I wanted. I wanted a person whose life would inspire me, who would make me love God more when I was with her. I wanted someone ahead of me in the work of guiding her children to know the Lord. I wanted a real friend—someone with whom I could enjoy life and have fun.

And while I could have licked my lonely wounds in isolation, God put it on my heart to seek friends as a hidden treasure. I should discover and cherish them—not sit around and wait for them to knock. So I kept my eyes out for women who were committed to and excited about their spiritual lives—perhaps a coworker, a mom who delighted in her children, or a community leader, a neighbor, someone more seasoned than me. I looked for people who already seemed to perceive themselves as "givers," who were seeking some way to invest their lives for others. Then I would simply ask them if they would want to meet for tea or coffee. I was almost never refused.

I actively sought someone who was giving of her own life, or who had a heart need that I could meet. Having someone as an inner circle friend meant looking for someone who would hit the ball back when I served it, so to speak. I looked for the women who had "life" about them. Because where Jesus is, there will be a sparkle, an excitement, a burning to want more of the deep things of God.

And so, I would almost always have to be the one who would make it happen. I would host lunches and teas, meet women for coffee, gather friends for long walks, and start small groups in my home, always searching for "excellent" women who would draw me to the best spiritual ideals. I learned this as a missionary in Poland. My house didn't need to be fancy or perfect, just open to potential friends. In reaching out to others and building a community, I found my best friends, sewing the threads of our lives together by serving in mutual ministries.

Initiating was not always simple, and hosting a tea often meant purposefully carving out space in the calendar. But I couldn't go it alone; I had to prioritize these relationships. I would call these women, send them notes or emails, and intentionally tell them the ways I admired them.

Take hold of that which is truly life.

1 TIMOTHY 6:19

In giving my life to others, often, God gave me the friends I so desperately needed. And now I have sisters in Christ all over the world who work, serve, and fellowship alongside me. We all support one another because we are devoted to one another's well-being. I just wish they all lived next door.

Relationships are an investment, and they require intentional giving and planning. Just as building a house requires plans and effort, so friendship grows out of intention and cultivation...and a firm foundation on the Rock that is Christ. Because when I follow the pattern of Jesus—calling my friends, meeting with them, teaching them, and serving them—then I follow His pattern of giving Himself.

TEATIME

Today, plan a simple teatime for someone you love. This isn't a time to fuss over the perfect decorations or an abundant spread. Tea biscuits (cookies!) from the cupboard might come in handy, along with cloth or pretty paper napkins and a special teacup. Find one or two details to signify that this is a special time—a time set apart. Invite your guest to choose a favorite teacup, brew a fresh pot, and sit together in companionship. But if you're looking for something to give an extra-special welcome, try a plate of baked goods, warm from the oven. I keep bags of cookie dough balls in my freezer so I can pop them in the oven whenever the occasion might arise.

But when there is time, nothing says "teatime" like fresh scones and raspberry jam! These scones are buttery, dense, and simple—and they'll be ready to dip in a cup of tea 20 minutes from now. This recipe is my staple for all kinds of gatherings, Bible studies, and table ministries.

Play with this recipe however you like. Add half a cup of cinnamon chips, chopped chocolate, raisins, cherries, or any combination of nuts and dried fruits. You can even add savory ingredients like ham, herbs, and grated cheese. Serve with hot tea, coffee, or lemonade.

My Favorite Scones

2 cups flour

4 tsp baking powder

1/4 tsp salt

1/3 cup sugar

(or cinnamon sugar, made of one part cinnamon to six parts sugar— I keep a jar of this ready for a little twist of flavor!)

6 Tbsp butter

3/4 cup heavy cream

1 egg

Preheat the oven to 375.

Mix together the flour, baking powder, salt, and sugar in a large bowl. Using two knives or a pastry blender, cut in the butter until you have a crumbly texture.

In a small bowl, beat the heavy cream and the egg. Stir this into the flour-butter mixture. At this point, you can also stir in any desired fillings.

Sprinkle flour on a counter and coat your hands. Shape the scone dough into a ball, and then flatten it into a disk. Cut the dough into eight wedges, place on a baking sheet, and bake 15 minutes, until golden in color.

1 cup heavy whipping cream

2 Tbsp sugar

1/2 tsp vanilla extract

Many of us know that clotted cream is slathered on scones in the UK. An easy substitute is whipped cream—which you can dress up any way you like.

If you have time, chill your mixing bowl and whisk in the freezer for a few minutes. A cold bowl gives the best whipped cream.

Using a hand or a stand mixer, whip the cream, sugar, and vanilla together on medium speed until stiff peaks form, 3 to 4 minutes. Spoon into a serving bowl.

If you'd like to play with this recipe, try adding an ounce of cream cheese or 1/8 tsp of almond extract. You could also substitute brown sugar or powdered sugar. And if you're looking for a colorful addition to your scones, stir in some chopped frozen berries once the cream is whipped.

Jesus is the Lover who reached out, initiated, poured out His love for our benefit. And so in friendship, I began to see myself as a giver of love, a builder of friendships, and an initiator of life.

LOVING YOUR PEOPLE WELL

*Would you like an adventure now...or would
you like to have your tea first?*

J.M. BARRIE, *Peter Pan*

Cobblestone roads threatened to trip me as I walked through crooked streets, which were sprinkled with potholes and dips here and there. I walked arm in arm with my dear friend as we explored an ancient village in the Cotswolds, and her support made me feel safe. Her patience with me as I walked slowly meant the world to my reticent heart as I forayed back into the world of walking and hiking. With a recent hip replacement, the last thing I wanted to do was fall. But the charming medieval village, with its blond brick cottages and shops, cafes, and teahouses galore, called our name and beckoned us to search out its treasures. My friend made these adventures possible for me.

The Cotswolds were famous for hundreds of years for having the finest wool; the sheep that made the industry possible flourished over acres and acres of grassy fields. And so, with endless miles of walking paths, we just *had* to walk among these curious animals and giggle at their antics.

Planning adventure days meant that, from time to time, my friend and I would put aside all duties and busyness

to make a memory, to explore, to find a new tea shop, or to seek out treasures in secondhand stores. Much of our lives are filled with duty, responsibility, work, and chores. Yet I have found that planning fun, taking adventures, and making joyful memories is one of the best ways to forge deep friendships and to keep your own heart filled. Laughter and tears are a vital part of growing close and deepening love that opens hearts to mutual influence. A true friend calls you to your best self, and friendship is the ground upon which discipleship best takes place. After all, relationship is at the core of influence.

My friend quite literally supported me as we explored the Cotswolds together, just as she provided emotional support in so many situations that came before. Over time, I had learned that my friend was a safe haven, a woman who created an atmosphere of love.

Time and Availability

Friendships develop better when you make your time together a priority. People grow close not through monitoring one another's behavior but by working together, playing together, talking together, celebrating together, and weeping together. Relationships develop when people are there for each other over time—and that's as true for parents and children as it is for anyone else.

Our influence is not only through our wise admonitions but also through intimacy built over time. Jesus lived day in, day out with His disciples. We see Him resting with them, walking, eating, mulling among crowds, teaching, and speaking in boats and at firesides over years. Heartfelt discipleship is not about fulfilling a formula, but about negotiating the ups and downs a real relationship creates.

Acceptance and Unconditional Love

In building meaningful relationships, we must learn to accept unconditionally the person God made each of us to be—even when the people in front of us have personality traits that differ from ours or that make us uncomfortable. Becoming a "safe" person, one who can be trusted, is important to the stability of the relationships. We need to accept the "warts" and irritating characteristics that may never change. Fortunately, they must see ours and learn to bear with us as well. We are called to love with a mature commitment that reaches past our feelings, which can change from circumstance to circumstance.

Often this means we must move beyond our prejudices, stretch to understand the heart behind a person's words, and seek to understand their context, their feelings, their thoughts, and the ways they look at life. We must make a commitment to sympathy, since understanding and compassion build bridges for love to be received.

Affirmation and Encouragement

I believe most people are acutely aware of their limitations and their failures. While we all need to grow to change, and correction of mistakes and even confrontation of our selfishness is necessary for growth, we also need recognition for our real efforts and accomplishments and positive reminders of who we can be with God's help.

You delight me. I am so grateful for you.
I am so blessed to have you as a friend.
You are my angel friend.
You put a smile in my heart.
I always have fun with you.
Thanks for always helping me.
You are one of the most encouraging, loving, spiritually sensitive, creative, diligent friends I have.

Grace

Everyone needs grace in order to grow. There are two verses that I have applied so many times in relationships that have opened a door to trust and the willingness to share secrets, fears, failures.

"Above all, keep fervent in your love for one another, because love covers a multitude of sins" (1 Peter 4:8). If anyone was familiar with fervent love amid seeming failure, it was Peter. He denied even knowing Jesus on the most important night in history, as He was facing crucifixion. And yet, through the fervent love of his Savior, Peter was restored to fellowship. What a beautiful picture! We are not called to point out all the flaws in the people around us but to graciously cover their downfalls when they need our grace and fervent love.

"A gentle answer turns away wrath, but a harsh word stirs up anger" (Proverbs 15:1). Over and over again, I have found there to be an invisible power in gentleness. When a friend or a child is filled with rage or anger, a humble response soothes the fury.

I'm sorry you're so discouraged.
I understand.
Nothing you can do will ever
separate you from my love.

A Set-Apart Space

In every bedroom in my home, you'll find a small table to hold a book, a candle, and two tea mugs. Two chairs are ready beside the table—just right for a quiet conversation in the morning or the evening, when the house is becoming still. Preparing rooms and furniture for conversations to naturally flow from life has served me over many years. I've been blessed to enjoy so many conversations at these tables—sharing confidences, offering thanksgiving, talking through problems, and celebrating God's blessings. These are the kinds of talks where true discipleship can take place, and where women can point each other straight to Jesus and His work in their lives. My marriage has been nurtured over such tables,

where grace is meted out amid stress. My children have been shaped through hours of conversation shared in the private place of one's room, where we can hide from the rest of our people for a few moments, sneaking a little space out from a large, loud, bubbling family.

Acts of Thoughtfulness and Kindness

I moved to Oxford several years ago. For years, I chatted with the barista at a neighborhood café, getting to know more details about her life little by little. The Lord put it on my heart to ask this young woman to my house for a cuppa. We chatted for about an hour. At the end of our time together, she said, "No one has ever asked me over to their house like this. I had so much fun today. I will never forget your kindness."

I could hardly believe her words. Later that year, my daughter and I surprised her with some small wrapped Christmas goodies. She said, "Oh, I'm spending Christmas alone. I will save your gifts until Christmas Day, and they will remind me of your friendship."

Acts of kindness speak volumes to someone of their worth to us. I am almost always surprised when someone takes time to show thoughtfulness to me in an actual way. A cup of tea, a handwritten card, some chocolate, a bunch of flowers, a "friend" date at a cafe, a long walk in a meadow or by a stream, a hike in the mountains, a back scratch or massage coupon, a trip to the park, a small gift, a surprise getaway from the difficulties of life, a planned adventure, or a ride with music blaring are all ways to say "I love you" to those we want to especially show our affection.

TEATIME

Years ago, my family and I took a short vacation for a few days in Devon, a sort of English Riviera. Medieval towns are sprinkled amid breathtaking beaches, cliffs, and national parks. Meandering from village to village, we came upon a little cafe at teatime, around three o'clock in the afternoon. Inside were small tables covered with lace tablecloths. A variety of teacups lined the shelves on the wall, and a spray of gorgeous flowers filled the small counter where a variety of glorious cakes were displayed. It was here that I first encountered coffee walnut cake. Such a heavenly, delectable treat.

This cake can be the centerpiece of an autumn teatime. You might also serve it with...

Warm mulled apple cider

Assorted cheeses—Brie, Gruyère, and a good aged Cheddar

Sliced Honeycrisp apples

Roasted, salted nuts

Savory crackers

Red and green grapes

A Cozy Harvest Tea Menu

Coffee Walnut Cake

1 cup (2 sticks) butter, softened

1 cup sugar

(I use natural, organic, unbleached sugar, but you can use regular)

2 tsp vanilla

4 eggs, slightly beaten

1/2 cup milk

1 1/2 cups unbleached white flour

2 tsp baking powder

1 1/4 tsp salt

2 Tbsp espresso powder

1 cup chopped walnuts

Preheat oven to 350.

Combine butter, sugar, and vanilla in large bowl and beat well. Add eggs and beat again until light and smooth. Stir in milk.

In a separate bowl, combine the flour, baking powder, salt, and espresso powder. Slowly fold dry ingredients into the egg mixture. Stir in chopped walnuts. Pour batter into a greased and floured Bundt pan or a 9 x 13 dish. Bake for 25 minutes, or until an inserted toothpick comes out clean.

Frost with your favorite vanilla frosting mixed with a tablespoon of brewed espresso.

Warm Mulled Apple Cider

1 gallon apple cider

4 cinnamon sticks

1 tsp whole cloves

1 orange, thinly sliced

1 1/2-inch piece fresh ginger, cut into 1/4-inch slices

Pour apple cider into a heavy-bottomed saucepan. Stir in cinnamon sticks, cloves, orange slices, and ginger slices. Bring to a simmer over medium heat, then reduce heat to low. Warm, stirring occasionally, until flavors have melded, about 30 minutes. Serve hot.

Two are better than one because they have a good return for their labor; for if either of them falls, the one will lift up his companion.

Ecclesiasties 4:9-10

PART TWO

THE HEART OF A FRIEND

As I have grown older, God has opened my eyes a little more each day to see the preciousness and fragility of our lives. Each day, I lean a little harder on Him. Each day, my confidence and faith for building my own life story rests a little less on my abilities and strengths as a woman, and more and more on God's character, love, and grace.

When we interact with others, they draw from what is invested inside ourselves. If wisdom, truth, and love have been built up as resources in our hearts, then when we encounter people, they will draw wisdom, truth, and love from the ways we speak to them and interact with them. People draw from what we have invested in our souls over years.

BREATH OF LIFE

A quiet secluded life in the country, with the possibility of being useful to people to whom it is easy to do good, and who are not accustomed to have it done to them; then work which one hopes may be of some use; then rest, nature, books, music, love for one's neighbor—such is my idea of happiness.

LEO TOLSTOY, *Family Happiness*

Somehow I managed to slip out of bed without waking Clay, slip on my shoes and a comfy sweater, and get out the door for a Saturday morning coffee. As I sat in the cozy corner of the cafe, coffee in hand, I basked in the delight of a stolen moment. I read my morning verses and jotted down some deep thoughts in my journal. *I will be so kind, very loving, and patient today*, I thought...I hoped.

And then my phone rang. "Mom! Where are you? What are we going to do today?" I responded patiently with this child—how could I not be patient in such a lovely moment?—and explained that I'd be home in just a little while to do something fun with the whole clan. Even just 30 minutes alone was rejuvenating for me.

But then the phone rang again. "Hey, honey! Who's going to take Joy downtown for her appointment?" This time it was my husband's voice. I pondered this. No less than four adults who could drive were in our home; perhaps one of them could manage? This was my one morning alone. Even so, I continued to talk with Clay as we puzzle-pieced schedules. As I ended the phone call, I breathed deeply. The coffee and quiet started to enchant my soul back into a pleasant attitude.

And then the phone rang. Again. Everyone was hungry and wanted breakfast. With another sigh, I gathered myself, thanked God for the few moments of peace, and resolved to enjoy the day and cherish my beloved ones, no matter what! This thought was barely a notion in my mind when I walked through the door to discover the dog had thrown up on the new carpet.

I think I need another cup of coffee.

So many times in my life I have encountered the tension between wanting to be Spirit-led and gracious and then being overwhelmed by my own attitudes, unexpected situations, or the many clashing personalities of my family members. Life tends to have a sandpaper effect on my attempts to be holy. These times have led me to explore what it means to live in the power of the Spirit. I cannot live a Christian life on my own power. I need the help, comfort, and gentle encouragement of God to keep growing every day. And this comes through His Spirit, who dwells within me.

Life tends to have a sandpaper effect on my attempts to be holy.

Throughout Scripture, the Holy Spirit is often described using the analogy of wind or breath. When explaining the mysteries of the Spirit to Nicodemus, Jesus says, "The wind blows where it wishes, and you hear the sound of it, but you do not know where it is coming from and where it is going; so is everyone who has been born of the Spirit" (John 3:8).

The Spirit might be described as...

...an inner strength. "God is our refuge and strength, a very ready help in trouble" (Psalm 46:1).

...a voice calling us to excellence. "The Helper, the Holy Spirit whom the Father will send in My name, He will teach you all things, and remind you of all that I said to you" (John 14:26).

...an energy moving us to love and forgive supernaturally. "The fruit of the Spirit is love" (Galatians 5:22).

...a fruitfulness that can only be explained by God. "I am the vine, you are the branches; the one who remains in Me, and I in him bears much fruit, for apart from Me you can do nothing" (John 15:5). When the Holy Spirit directs our course, the natural consequence is a life outside of normal striving or fleshly effort. We are able to live beyond our own capacity.

The Greek word Jesus uses is *pnuema*, which can be translated as wind, breath, or spirit. Later, when Jesus is commissioning His disciples, Scripture manifests the metaphor into an actual happenstance: "When He had said this, He breathed on them and said to them, 'Receive the Holy Spirit'" (John 20:22).

Breath is a daily necessity. We cannot live without breathing. It is a constant need. The same sort of dependence we have on breathing is how we ought to depend on the Holy Spirit. Living in the power of the Holy Spirit means letting the Spirit of God be the breath that carries us through every day. Relying on the assistance of the Holy Spirit should become as natural to us as breathing in and out.

CONVERSATION AND CONTEMPLATION

God told His people to rest—to devote time every week to worship and soul-filling activities. Why do we, today, still need to set apart times for peace and rest during our daily work?

What are the rhythms, habits, and routines that fill you with peace amid all your responsibilities? How could you cultivate these peaceful moments more intentionally? What do you need emotionally to build deep friendships into the rhythms of your life?

_____

_____

_____

_____

_____

_____

_____

_____

_____

_____

_____

_____

_____

_____

_____

_____

Lord, fill me with Your Spirit today, now. Teach me to walk with You, to see my life from Your perspective, and give me the strength to grow. Help me to worship You as I live this day.

FEASTING ON GOD'S GRACE

I believe in Christianity as I believe that the Sun has risen, not only because I see it, but because by it I see everything else.

C.S. LEWIS, *The Weight of Glory*

Many years ago, living as a missionary in Austria, I attended a Christmas party hosted by dear friends and team members of the organization with whom I worked. At this event, our friends spoke to all of us about Christ as the ultimate gift.

Standing in a corner was a young Austrian woman I had invited who worked as my friend's au pair. Claudia could hardly have looked less engaged in the message being shared. I turned toward her, attempting conversation in my halting German. We barely shared a language, but before we parted, I managed to invite her to a nearby cafe for a cup of tea and a pastry later in the month.

When she arrived, we feasted on *Milchrahmstrudel*, a Viennese specialty. We poured the hot vanilla sauce over the cream cheese and ricotta pastry. The sharing of a treat seemed to put her at ease and open her heart. I asked questions and listened to her story. Having grown up in a small village in the Austrian Alps, she was an only child. She had very little exposure to issues of faith, but the mountain beauty, forests, and grassy hills had spoken to her of a creator. Before we left, I pressed a German Bible into her hands. "This is a gift," I said.

The next week, I saw her again. She came up to me with a sparkle in her eyes and showed me the Bible, already dog-eared and underlined. "I hope I've been doing the right thing," she told me. "I've been reading this every day. I want to know God. I have wanted this for many years."

Knowing that my German language was so limited and my spiritual vocabulary so sparse, I did not expect that she had understood anything of our conversation. I had grossly underestimated how God could use me despite my limitations. Yet early in her journey as a follower of Jesus, this young woman seemed to know instinctively what it means to seek God. She was thirsty for His messages, the whispers of His love. The Bible I gave her was a resource she had been wanting. She told me she had longed for a relationship with God but that no one had ever been able to explain it to her.

A long time ago, I came to Christ because a complete stranger took the initiative to share Christ with me. I was a college freshman

living on the tenth floor of a dorm, secretly praying, *If there is a God in the universe, can You please make Yourself known to me?* I deeply longed for love and purpose. On the outside, no one knew or observed my desperate prayers. The meeting with the Austrian woman reminded me of this. There are people in each of our lives who have never heard or understood the love, forgiveness, and grace of God. How important it is that we reach out to those who have such longings. And sharing a cup of tea, a meal, or a treat is often the way to open hearts.

Perhaps you are like me, naturally reticent or shy to share Christ with others. But I often think how different my life would have been if the shy girl who knocked on my door had not taken the initiative to talk to me. Extending friendship, hospitality, and love is the pathway to the opportunity to share His life-giving messages.

Start with Prayer

Prayer is simply turning your heart toward God to commune with Him. Praying from the heart means coming to God as you are, without pretense, and lifting your thoughts, burdens, struggles, requests, and hopes to Him. Through this practice, you acknowledge that you believe God exists, that He listens, and that He will respond to you personally. Ask God to make you aware of those around you who need a touch of His grace, a word of encouragement, or a moment of focused friendship amid the busy moments of your days.

Prayer opens your heart to the grace of God in a way nothing else can. In prayer, you experience His presence and His personal involvement in your life—the life of God intersecting your own. You need the grace of His life living in your heart in order to serve

the women who come across your doorstep; the child who needs your love, wisdom, and reassurance; and the spouse or roommate who needs some gentle sympathy. For me, prayer is not a larger-than-life emotional experience. It is more of a habit of turning my heart to God and asking Him to intervene in the moments of my day, then seeking to be sensitive to His quiet voice in my moments. So feed on God's grace in prayer, and then live out the reality that comes from living in companionship with Him.

Discover the Word

The truth of Scripture is food for your mind—spiritual nourishment for growing in maturity, faith, and wisdom.

If prayer is you speaking to God, then by reading the Bible, you'll experience God speaking to you. I believe God's message, through Scripture, is the vocabulary the Holy Spirit uses to speak to us throughout the moments of our days. The truth of Scripture is food for your mind—spiritual nourishment for growing in maturity, faith, and wisdom. God's Word is "living and active," and it goes deep into your "soul and spirit" (Hebrews 4:12). It is "inspired by God and beneficial" for all that will make you mature (2 Timothy 3:16). Scripture is God revealing His mind and heart to you, teaching you to be His follower, explaining spiritual realities, and guiding you with wisdom for every situation. In a world teeming with false truths and foolish values, we need the direction and wisdom that God's Word gives us every day.

"Mama, how do you know so much about God? It seems like He is your friend," my little one commented one day. What a joy to say that God *is* my friend! I slowly acquired an organic, living understanding of Him through years of resting in His reality every day.

He was my Father, my friend, my confidant, my counselor, my teacher, my joy. It happened little by little, season by season—as all relationships do. Maturity comes in spiritual life as it comes in our actual lives, a bit at a time over years.

It's helpful to remember that every Christian is called to be a disciple. In the Gospels—the first four books of the New Testament that tell the stories of Christ's life, ministry, death, and resurrection—the word *disciple* is often used simply to describe those who were students of Jesus, their teacher. And the word *Christian* means "Christ in one." So growing as a believer in Him means He is at the center of our thoughts, actions, and values. It is not just a religious practice but an authentic relationship. We read and ponder the stories He shared. We observe the ways He treated others. From this understanding, we seek to please Him. We obey His commands. We grow in our compassion for others as Christ exhibited Himself.

Read through the first four books of the New Testament—Matthew, Mark, Luke, and John. Take time to meditate and journal on the passages and stories where Jesus describes the qualities, behavior, and character of His faithful followers. As you grow in knowledge as a follower, you can also grow as one who can share wisdom and lead others to Him.

Let's consider how to encourage one another in love and good deeds, not abandoning our own meeting together, as is the habit of some people, but encouraging one another.

HEBREWS 10:24-25

Love Those Around You

By personality, I am a lover of people. Spending time with my adult children, having a cup of tea and sharing companionship with my husband, and talking to a long-cherished friend over brunch are some of my favorite things to do. I *love* my people. We are made for love; we thrive best where we have community—someone who see us, who cares for our thoughts and feelings, who is willing to invest the treasure of time with us.

One of the things I love and appreciate most about Christ is that He is relational too. He lived His story on earth through companionship with real people—friends, His disciples, children, prostitutes, and misfits. His influence wasn't just espousing a doctrine or theology to be memorized; it was a real-time interaction of eating, walking, talking, looking at the stars He had thrown into place, walking among the flowers of the field, and taking notice.

So the Christian life is not just about what we know but also how we feel, what we do, how we think, how we relate, and what we enjoy. And all of us were made for love, life, and community as a part of the reality of Christ among us.

I know many women long for friendship and companionship in this isolationist world. From moving 19 times—6 times internationally—I understand loneliness. Yet I have found that I often have to be the one who invites, who welcomes, who initiates the very fellowship I need and long for. When women seek out and cultivate fellowship, a community thrives.

Recently, I spent a few days with my grandchildren. Whatever Lilian, the three-year-old, did, Samuel, her little brother mimicked. Whatever she said, he said. Whatever she had, he wanted! They obviously are rubbing off on each other.

So it is with Christ. And with friends. He rubs off on us, then we rub off on others from spending time with Him. We become like those we hang around with.

Jesus showed the world what God is really like. The more time we invest in our relationship with Him, the more we allow His presence, His stories, and His reality to become a part of our being. And the more we become like Christ, the more we mimic His reality to others, showing a needy world what love is like.

A disciple is, at her core, a dedicated learner who follows the teacher. She models the teacher in all she does; her actions flow not from mere obedience to laws or culture, but from the heart and her relationship with the teacher. Through witnessing her life, others will experience the teacher's message for themselves. A disciple wants to soak in everything she can about the message and the teacher! So in the same way you learn from God by reading and studying His words on your own, you also learn from others who feed on Scripture and then share what they learned in spoken messages and written books. Their insightful words can inspire, instruct, explain, explicate, and expand on the truths in God's Word in ways you might miss. When you listen to or read the words of others who study and think deeply about God's Word and the life of faith, you are nourished by the overflow of their maturity, wisdom, and insight; your mind is strengthened and sharpened by their words. Let me invite you to feed on God's truth in the messages, books, and writings of other godly believers you respect.

When you fellowship with other godly believers who are feeding on God's gracious, generous love, you are nourished by the

He is the radiance of [God's] glory and the exact representation of His nature.

HEBREWS 1:3

overflow of their spirits, and your heart is spiritually encouraged and strengthened in their presence. And, even better, you can become that source of life and encouragement to someone else.

Lone ranger women who depend on no one but themselves, relying on their own strength, are more prone to giving up, giving in to depression, and quitting their ideals. We weren't made to live in isolation. The faith of believers around you feeds your faith and fills your heart. Timothy received that same kind of grace from his friend and mentor Paul, and Paul had Barnabas, the "Son of Encouragement," as a source of grace in his life. You need that gift of encouragement in your life too. Find a godly friend or mentor who will pray for you and encourage you, and make time to spend time with them. If you are in a place where you do not have a local spiritual friend, call someone long-distance. Find a mentor on a podcast that calls you to your best self, where you feel understood and led. Read books that fill your heart and soul. Let all of these, from the spiritual community, nourish your spirit.

Remember, you cannot offer God's living water to anyone if your own spiritual well has run dry. You cannot be a faith-forming influence on others if your own faith is not being formed. Be sure you are being refreshed and nourished by God's grace and truth so that you, in turn, will be able to refresh and nourish others.

Today, find a corner of your home just for yourself. Sit in a cozy chair, cover your lap with a favorite blanket, and light a candle or two. Take a few moments to brew a cup of your favorite tea, and when you sit down, envision yourself as one of Jesus's disciples. Reflect on what it means to follow Him, listen to Him, and steep yourself in His Word. You are free to share your fears, your doubts. Spend time in prayer and intimacy with the One who knows you best.

We reflect Christ...

...in our touch, a warm embrace.

...in our words. "Welcome. I am so happy to be with you today."

...in our actions. "Come, let's have some tea and a berry crumble. I've prepared a quiet place where we can relax."

...in serving. "I know this is a challenging time for your family. I would love to bring you a meal."

TEATIME

A hot cup of tea on a cold day is delightful, but when the weather's warm, take time to go outside and delight in God's creation. You might read or journal on your porch, take a long walk with a friend, or invite some women to join you in a warm-weather teatime.

Mango Iced Tea

Blueberry Crumb Cake

Chocolate-Covered Almonds

Quiet Time Outdoors

Mango Iced Tea

1 cup frozen or fresh mango, chopped
2 cups pineapple juice
8 bags green tea
2 fresh mint sprigs
4 cups boiling water
1/4 cup sugar

Blend the mango and pineapple juice in a blender until smooth. Set aside in the refrigerator to chill for 10 minutes.

Place tea bags and mint in a large pitcher. Pour boiling water over the top and let steep for 5 minutes. Remove mint and tea bags, then stir in the sugar and chilled mango mixture. Stir until smooth and pour into ice-filled glasses. Garnish with a slice of mango and a mint leaf.

Blueberry Crumb Cake

Topping

5 Tbsp flour
1/2 cup sugar
1 tsp cinnamon
1/8 tsp salt
1/4 cup butter

Cake

1/4 cup butter
3/4 cup sugar
Zest of 1 lemon
1 egg
1/2 cup milk
1 tsp vanilla
Scant 2 cups flour
2 tsp baking powder
1/2 tsp salt
1 pint fresh blueberries

Heat oven to 375. Grease a 9-inch round or springform baking pan.

Prepare the topping: Combine the flour, sugar, cinnamon, and salt. Using a fork or a pastry blender, cut in butter until the mixture is combined into coarse crumbs. Set aside.

In a large bowl, beat butter, sugar, and lemon zest together until light and fluffy. Add egg, milk, and vanilla and beat until combined. Stir in flour, baking powder, and salt. Fold blueberries into the batter.

Spoon batter into prepared pan. Scatter crumbs over the top. Bake 40 minutes, or until a toothpick inserted into the center comes out clean. Let cool completely before serving.

HOPE WHEN YOU FEEL DISCOURAGED

Where there's hope, there's life. It fills us with
fresh courage and makes us strong again.

ANNE FRANK, *The Diary of a Young Girl*

What do you do when life doesn't come close to the way you believe it should look? Perhaps the vision you have for your home and for the influence you'll have there is so far from your reality that you have no idea how to reconcile the two, and discouragement and frustration have started to seep in. There's never enough of you to go around, and you can't even cover the basics—much less enjoy the riches of the ministry God has entrusted to you!

Don't give up! Hope for the best. You have enormous work ahead of you—loving, ministering, and shaping your faith and the faith of those around you. This work is especially challenging in an isolationist culture that provides few support systems. This same culture offers so much differing advice, bringing voices into our heads that inevitably produce feelings of guilt and inadequacy. Feelings, though, are never the same as God's truth. When you're overwhelmed by the task ahead, remind yourself of these truths.

1. God is with me, and He will help me succeed.

Each of us experiences "winter" seasons in our lives—times when growth is stagnant, when our dreams appear to be dead and buried. But while we can hardly perceive it at the time, roots are growing deep in these seasons.

I have experienced all the realities of discouraging seasons. Yet through the eyes of faith, I can see how God shaped me, guided me, and grew me through each. As a matter of fact, it was in my winter seasons—times when I was humbled, failed to live up to my own expectations, and felt my circumstances were out of control—that I actually learned the wisdom and compassion that others in my life would need. My own failures and weaknesses have cultivated compassion and sympathy in my heart for others struggling as I have. None of us can relate to a perfect person, but those who understand our frailties and struggles are much more likely to be our friends.

If you are in a winter season, rest in the knowledge that while we are not adequate to do God's work by ourselves, God's Spirit is working behind the scenes in our midst. He will take all we have to give Him within our own limitations, and our offering of ourselves becomes enough. Remember the little boy who gave all that he had to feed 5,000 people? He gave his basket of fives loaves of bread and two fish—hardly enough to feed the gigantic crowd! And yet in God's hands, the offering was more than enough.

> *If God is for us, who is against us?*
> **ROMANS 8:31**

Give what you have and trust God to fill in the rest. Daily, I ask God to make up for my shortcomings, and by faith I live as though what God promised is true. If your heart is to serve Him, He is for you. He has compassion on you, He knows your weariness, and He is your champion.

2. There are always do-overs in God's economy.

All of us mess up. Peter blew it royally when he denied Christ at His hour of need, but before he even sinned, Jesus told Peter He had prayed for him. Jesus had compassion on Peter before His disciple had even committed his sinful act.

Where do we get this illusion that we're supposed to be perfect? Don't be so hard on yourself; disappointed expectations only sap your strength further. In this fallen world, we will never be able to control ourselves, our families, our circumstances, or the people around us. But we live in grace and, little by little, move toward maturity. Live in the grace and knowledge that God forgives, knows your limitations, and is not surprised or disappointed by your lack.

There is now no condemnation at all for those who are in Christ Jesus.

ROMANS 8:1

3. A wise woman learns her limitations.

We read the story of the prophet Elijah defeating the priests of Baal in the book of 1 Kings. But just after this victory, Elijah was so weary from the spiritual battle that he despaired of his life, wishing he hadn't been born. God saw Elijah's exhaustion, and mercifully, God gave the prophet rest. "He lay down and fell asleep under a broom tree," says 1 Kings 19:5, "but behold, there was an angel touching him, and he said to him, 'Arise, eat!'" This angel came as a personal healer, feeding Elijah with a loaf of bread and a comforting touch instead of a lecture.

Sometimes women go so long without taking a break that they start breaking down. Wise women learn to say no so they don't live in a constant state of exhaustion. As a person in ministry, I want to be available to everyone. But I can't meet the needs of everyone in my surroundings and still have peace in my home. Since I can only hold onto so many ideals at once, I choose to hold onto the ones that matter most. I regularly review and plan what I can reasonably do and still move toward a flourishing, sustainable life. Sometimes this planning must happen every month.

We are not just minds and hearts; we are bodies with limitations. When we overexert, we crash and burn! Taking care of our bodies is essential to our emotional, spiritual, and physical well-being. If you're tired, give yourself sleep and nourishing foods. Surround yourself with beauty to remind you of what you're worth—whatever *beauty* means for you. Maybe it's a meandering stroll through a local nursery or a used bookshop, an hour putting watercolors to canvas, or making music on a long-neglected instrument. You are worth being cared for, so take responsibility for your happiness and well-being. Managing my own happiness and sense of joy is not frivolous; it is a necessity. My friends, children, colleagues, and husband prefer a happy, content companion. No one else is responsible for this. If I am to be wise and mature, I must monitor myself, that I may refuel and live in the real world as a gift of grace, love, and strength to others. As life empties me, I have placed rhythms in my days and weeks where I may fill back up.

Bless the LORD, my soul,
And do not forget any of His benefits...
Who satisfies your years with good things,
So that your youth is renewed like the eagle.

PSALM 103:2, 5

4. I can seek outside perspective.

You might need some inspiration and counsel in order to move forward. Find someone older, wiser, and more experienced to help you come up with a plan. Sometimes this is easier said than done! But I have found that when I summon the courage to pour out my heart to more mature believers, I usually find compassion and often find help.

For many years, I found mentorship through books. I love reading the words of seasoned, experienced believers who have gone before me. I constantly seek to read, educate myself, and find models

When my anxious thoughts multiply within me,
Your comfort delights my soul.

PSALM 94:19

of wisdom and integrity. As a disciple of God, I am a learner, and I am determined to learn and grow in wisdom every year. Reach out to others to start a book club or a small group study that you might become strengthened together. It is a great way to make friendships—gathering around great thoughts, sharing lives... *friendship.*

5. I can pace myself.

If you're feeling overwhelmed at the tasks ahead, ask yourself what's stealing your peace of mind. What's sapping your energy, and how can you make a change? What in your life is not producing good fruit? Your overcomplicated schedule? Your lack of rhythms and consistent habits? Comparing yourself to others? Listening to voices that bring false guilt or accuse you of inadequacy? Putting your finger on what's *not* working is the first step to making positive change.

One who walks with wise people will be wise.

PROVERBS 13:20

Commit to identifying the stressors and drainers over which you have control and, as much as possible, eliminating them. Be honest about what needs to go and vigilant about removing it from your life. Say no! Limit yourself; don't accept responsibilities out of guilt. Instead, be disciplined about pursuing the godly wisdom that provides peace and good fruit.

What inspires your heart, gives you a break, and helps to keep you going a little bit longer? And as you consider the new decisions that will keep you from being overwhelmed, remember that a disciple of Jesus dedicates herself to worship.

As a father has compassion on his children,
So the LORD has compassion on those who fear Him.
For he Himself knows our form;
He is mindful that we are nothing but dust.

PSALM 103:13-14

6. I can give the day to God.

First things first! Beginning the day with the Lord will orient you. Set yourself on the right path for the hours ahead, with God's truth and wisdom casting light over your priorities and plans. I always commit to beginning the day with devotions, worship, and reading. Even if I don't get anything else accomplished in the day—even if every plan is sidetracked—I've praised the Lord, I've thanked Him for His mercies, and I've poured out my heart to Him.

In the morning, LORD, You will hear my voice;
In the morning I will present my prayer to You and be on the watch.

PSALM 5:3

When I find myself walking a dark, discouraging path, these are still the truths and habits that sustain me. Proverbs 4:18 tells us, *"The path of the righteous is like the light of dawn. That shines brighter and brighter until the full day."*

Every day, a little more light. Every day, a little more progress. And one day, true brightness—the brightness of the Son. So don't give in to discouragement or feelings of inadequacy. You are more capable than you know, and you are the right one to handle and shape your life's story. You are precious to God, and through the trials you endure, He guides you, nurtures you, and makes you strong. If you leave your burdens in His hands, the God who began a good work in you will—in His time, little by little—complete it.

God loves you; God is *for you*—so who can be against you? God is a compassionate Father who forgives every shortcoming in your life.

TEATIME

Teatime for me isn't just a morning ritual. I'll daily have a cuppa in the middle of the afternoon. On the busiest days, this brings a few minutes of quiet when I can sit still, catch my breath, and center again. I have passed on this habit to each of my children; Clay and I have practiced it for years to keep our daily sanity and equilibrium.

Busy women need these moments. Like you, I've often started the day off on the wrong foot, gotten irritated at something silly, ranted and raved about it, rushed around too much instead of working margin into my day, griped and complained, and offended my family. I have failed often in the presence of those I love most. I've had to admit my inability and cast myself on grace alone.

When my heart gets grouchy, wisdom has taught me to look at what is bubbling inside. What is causing such conflict? I head to my tea cupboard and get out a real china cup. While the water boils, I select the perfect tea bag and gather the sugar and milk. And then, while the tea steeps, I wait. This time is a necessary pause, and as I count the moments, I quiet my heart. I confess all the ways I've tried to operate in my own strength and found myself lacking. And I invite the Holy Spirit to move in me— giving me the patience, understanding, and joy I cannot summon on my own.

The tea, now, is perfectly steeped. I add the milk, stir in the sugar, and drink. And I don't just have a surge of caffeine, but an experience, an event in my day—a chance to *save* the day.

When Your Heart Gets Grouchy

Chai Tea

1 star anise pod

1/2 tsp whole cloves

1/2 tsp whole allspice

2 sticks cinnamon

1 cardamom pod, crushed

2 cups water

4 cups milk

3 bags black tea

*(such as English breakfast) or
1 heaping Tbsp loose-leaf tea*

Honey, to taste

In a saucepan, combine spices and water. Bring to a boil, then remove from heat and let steep for 5 minutes.

Add milk and bring mixture to a simmer. Remove from heat and add tea. Let steep for 5 to 20 minutes. (A longer steep will give a stronger flavor.)

Remove the tea bags and strain the spices out of the mixture. Reheat if desired and sweeten with honey to taste. This recipe makes enough to share—or to save for the next time you need a luxurious treat.

A FEW OF MY
FAVORITE THINGS

"Do you just drink tea and light candles all the time? When do you get everything *done?*"

I had to laugh when I heard the question. Far from slowing down, life has gotten busier with every year I age! Between ministry commitments, deadlines, family needs, and a near-endless list of projects I dream of accomplishing, *busy* (or at least *full on*) seems to characterize my every day. Why shouldn't I take the time to light candles, listen to music, and savor a cup of tea? Why shouldn't I balance all that busyness with a moment of peace in the middle of my day?

Even 15 minutes of that intentional time will fill me up again, equipping my heart and spirit to continue the work of the day. This endless cycle of giving, filling up, and giving again is necessary for a home to flourish. I intentionally step back and enjoy a few favorite things...

Lovely music. I'll often reach for the soundtracks of *Pride and Prejudice, Miss Potter,* or *Ladies in Lavender.* I'm likewise inspired by Celtic rhythms and the music of film scores.

Good food. Whether it's a salad with avocados, onions, and nuts (always lots of nuts!), a handful of dark chocolates, or a plate of old-fashioned chocolate chip cookies or Hob Knobs, good food gives me more than just physical energy. Even a nibble can be a feast—an opportunity to express delight and give God gratitude.

Inspiring films and shows. I love immersing myself in English dramas, romances, and mysteries. I'll often turn to adaptations of old classics like *Pride and Prejudice, Sense and Sensibility, David Copperfield, Lark Rise to Candleford,* and *Wives and Daughters.*

Beautiful and thought-provoking magazines. These grace many of our coffee tables and book baskets. *Victoria* magazine is an old favorite with home ideas and featuring artists, authors, recipes, and nature photography—a lovely inspiration for shaping beauty at home. *Plough* magazine is filled with inspiring articles, also beautiful in design.

Old tales, well told. I'm always on the lookout for books that paint delightful pictures of life-giving homes. Whether I'm listening to an audiobook, reading to myself, or reading aloud with my family, the charm of lovely stories and beautiful language never disappoints.

- Elizabeth Goudge is a favorite storyteller. *Pilgrim's Inn* is my favorite of her tales!
- Other favorites of mine are biographies of great people as well as historical fiction.
- We read the stories of James Herriot aloud to our children—usually during Sunday afternoon tea. The stories—as well as the television series based on them—are warm, joyful, and surprisingly funny.
- Good books for children are even better when shared! Common read-alouds in our home include *The Little Princess* and

The Secret Garden, both by Frances Hodgson Burnett; *Anne of Green Gables* and its sequels by Lucy Maude Montgomery; *Cheaper by the Dozen* by Ernestine Gilbreth Carey; and the Chronicles of Narnia by C.S. Lewis. The beloved Lord of the Rings trilogy by J.R.R. Tolkien never disappoints.

- For instruction and inspiration, I often turn to the books of Eugene Peterson, Philip Yancey, and Henri Nouwen's *The Life of the Beloved.*

A wise woman takes care of her soul, and all these small pleasures equip me to flourish and continue the work of the day. Make space for the activities that bring joy to your soul, whatever they are, and let God use them to show you His beauty, comfort, and delight.

*Let Your favor, L*ORD*, be upon us,*
Just as we have waited for You.
Psalm 33:22

A DECLUTTERED SOUL

*The architect should strive continually to simplify; the
ensemble of the rooms should then be carefully considered that
comfort and utility may go hand in hand with beauty.*

FRANK LLOYD WRIGHT

We are, in a sense, architects of our own souls. We have agency and power to direct what is contained there, what is to be thrown away. The foundations we build on determine the strength and stability of our lives.

In the real world, we can all see how too much clutter in our rooms and too many piles of *things* cause us to feel overwhelmed. Slowly, I have learned to declutter, to simplify, as often as I can. Clay is really the master at this when it comes to our home. He helps me get rid of what's not needed and organize what we need to keep around. He recently decluttered our pantry—threw away chip bags that held little but took up space, cleared out empty water bottles and junky Christmas candy that would never be eaten, hung baskets that had fallen off their nails, and put away groceries that had never been put in their place. Now, if someone came into my pantry, they would mistakenly think I'm an organized person. (Thank goodness for Clay!) It made me feel good just to open the door and see that all is manageable again.

I have come to realize my brain and heart can be the same

way—cluttered with worries, responsibilities, duties, finances, time constraints, expectations, disappointments, critical attitudes, resentment, and grief. I have stored up distinct sadness, confusion, disappointment, and occasionally anger that need to be dealt with. All these added together tend to create soul piles and mind clutter. If I don't take the time to sort the piles, my spirit becomes a mess and my heart becomes overwhelmed and weary.

Each day brings an opportunity to make a new plan, to simplify the mind messes. In the same way that clearing out closets brings me relief, soul and mind decluttering brings me rest, equipping me to face each day in peace. So I come to the place where I know I will find the help I need. I come to God and ask Him to help me, His child, and ask Him how to clean out and organize my soul. He can help me get rid of the junk that is unnecessary, that burdens my thoughts and feelings and leave peace in its place.

God speaks to me gently as I seek to identify and unearth all the pressures, fears, and burdens I am carrying. I list all my soul-clutter piles in my journal—worries, sinful attitudes, bitterness, fears, and issues that will suck me and my energy dry. Prayerfully, I place them in the file drawer of heaven and leave them there. He never wearies of carrying what I am not capable of holding.

"Only one thing is necessary," Jesus told Martha (Luke 10:42). So many priorities and worries offer us ways to feel guilty or ill-equipped, but we don't have to make choices that will add unnecessary pressure or cause us to grumble in sin. When we seek after Jesus, giving Him our calendars, our thoughts, our loyalty, we will free ourselves from burdens He never meant us to carry. As I yield my lists to God, and even as my house comes to order when I clean and straighten long-neglected cupboards, my soul, too, moves in the direction of order.

If you also long for a decluttered soul, find a quiet space. Brew a pot of tea. And ask yourself these questions:

- Is any guilt or unconfessed sin festering in your heart? Admit to God that you need Him, desiring His grace and forgiveness. The older I get, the more I understand humility as central to finding peace. I admit my mistakes, lightening the weight of my soul.
- Are there any hurts, burdens, fears, or worries that you are carrying on your own shoulders? Write them down, give them over into God's hands, and ask for practical wisdom about how to handle them. Pray from your heart about how you need help.

- Are you carrying any bitterness? Is cynicism stealing your joy? Are you a person who repeatedly has a critical attitude toward everyone, including yourself? When we do not offer forgiveness or accept the limitations of a circumstance or person, we are the ones who suffer. Bitterness poisons our soul. Be humble. Give up your desire for revenge; don't succumb to the temptations of a gossiping heart and mouth. Accept people in the context of their lives. Accept yourself in the context of your own demanding story.

Even as we might sort out a closet—throw away outdated and used clothing, papers, books, toys, or unnecessary items—so we need to sort our feelings, thoughts, spirit, body, and life. We need to throw out unneeded items in order to make a fresh start. Too often in the demands of life, we carry burdens inside that we are not even aware of. These burdens keep us from living in the freedom, peace, and love God intended us to experience every day. But it takes time and intentionality to take off burdens, to wash our hearts clean, and to move forward with the grace and energy God wants us to know. But we can pursue joy—just as God intends!

"In quietness and trust is your strength," God says in Isaiah 30:15. And later in Scripture, Jesus offers this invitation: "Come to Me, all who are weary and burdened, and I will give you rest. Take My yoke upon you and learn from Me, for I am gentle and humble in heart, and you will find rest for your souls" (Matthew 11:28-29). Only God can give us what we need. Only He is the source of rest and peace. I can quiet my soul and wait on His timing. There's no need to force an issue or beg God to hurry up. He is sovereign; I can be calm.

PRAYER

DEAR HEAVENLY FATHER,

I come to You today, thanking You that You are the God who gives us peace—grateful that nothing can separate us from Your love, that You are compassionate and generous of heart to us, Your children.

Please, Lord, grant these precious ones the ability to off-load their burdens, fears, and worries into Your capable hands. Let them find rest and comfort in You, no matter what their situation. And most of all, let them move through the moments of their days with Your peace, Your strength, and a real knowledge and experience of Your unconditional love.

In Jesus's precious name, we come to Your throne of grace.

AMEN.

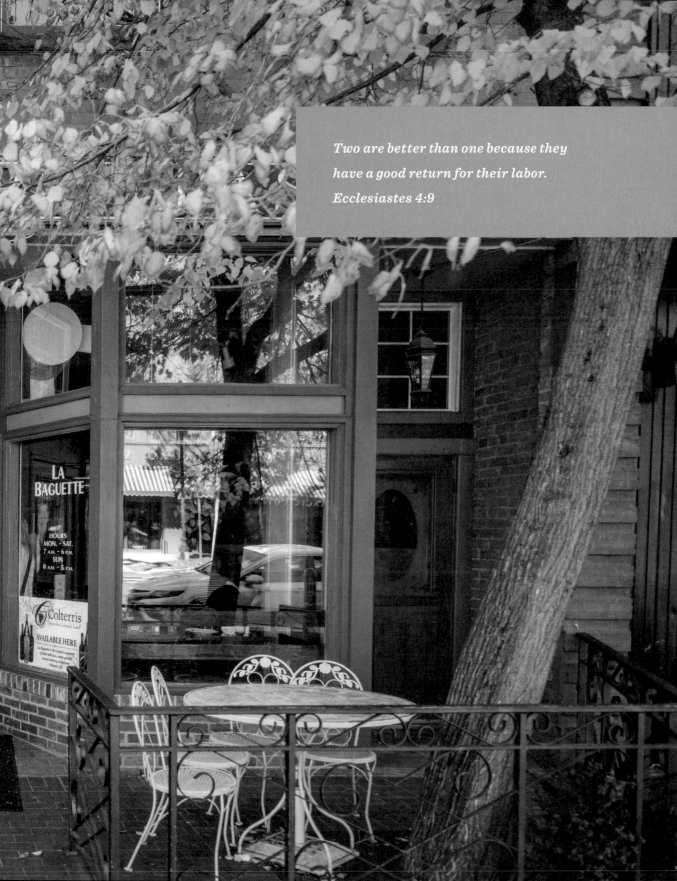

Two are better than one because they have a good return for their labor.
Ecclesiastes 4:9

PART THREE

LIGHT A CANDLE

Women who choose hope and choose to trust God are those who, instead of cursing the darkness, light a candle. But this is a conscious act of will. Hope is not a feeling; it is a commitment to hold fast to what Scripture reminds us is true about God. Knowing God's Word, pondering it, and truly taking it into the soul is what gives each of us fuel to live the Christian life. May we listen as the Holy Spirit guides us through the wisdom we have learned. The only way to live well is in fellowship with God. Nothing else will satisfy.

A FIRE OF LOVE
AND PURPOSE

We cannot tell the precise moment when friendship is
formed. As in filling a vessel drop by drop, there is at last a
drop which makes it run over; so in a series of kindnesses
there is at least one which makes the heart run over.

RAY BRADBURY, *Fahrenheit 451*

A small coffee shop in an obscure neighborhood in War-
saw, Poland, became a place of forever inspiration for me.
Sitting with a beloved friend, one of the first women in our
ministry outreach in Poland, I longed to unearth thoughts
deeply influencing her unusual fervor for Christ. Her commitment to Him had cost her greatly. She had been ques-
tioned several times by the secret police and had borne
years of financial challenge while seeking to live on a small
salary. She didn't want to work long hours; she wanted to
preserve time in her daily calendar to encourage women
around her.

Sacrificing so much to live as a believer in a Communist
country, she pressed forward knowing that persecution
and difficulty lay ahead.

Why?

"I learned that Jesus is the King of the universe," she

said. "As His child, I understood that because I was related to Him, I was a princess, royalty, personal worth, something I never found in Communism. That gives me great value as a human being. I never found that sense of self anywhere else. Living as God's child gives me purpose, meaning, forever love."

We long to know our lives can make a real difference—that our being alive and making right choices isn't just a duty but also a heart-gripping reality that will make a purposeful impact in the lives of others. Jesus called His disciples away from their tasks to make an imprint on history.

Come, follow Me, and I will send You out to fish for people.

Go and make disciples of all nations.

These uneducated men have turned the world upside-down.

Paul and Peter willingly, even joyfully, sacrificed their lives because they saw themselves having a part in God's great story. Perhaps in the dogged system of taxes, Roman rule, and poverty abounding, they longed to know something in their lives mattered—just as we do. They knew they had value, that they were part of the movement of the Spirit of God to redeem the world for their Creator. Service without heart deadens the soul, but the love and passion in their hearts gave them the motivation to serve.

And so, when we seek to encourage and personally affirm those who come across our path, we are cultivating in them an understanding of their great worth to Christ. We are instilling within them a hope that they, with their unique personalities, skills, and circumstances, are playing a part.

Theology—knowledge of God—is not just about storing doctrine
in our minds, but also lighting a fire of love and purpose
as we know and grow in relationship to Christ.

That's what discipleship is—captivating hearts with a passion for Christ and teaching others to commune with Him through the seasons of their lives. Discipleship, then, is not about indoctrination. Discipleship is about the heart. So now is the time for Christians—the Christ ones—to emulate His greatness, excellence, beauty, civility, redemption, care, and truth that conquers all.

When women are filled with the power, love, wisdom, and celebration of the Spirit, the next generation will catch the fire of their passion. What about you? Can you lean into the strength, wisdom, love, and gentleness of your sweet Savior and then come out of His presence giving a fragrance of His reality?

Discipling others is not about authority, great faith, strong personality, spiritual giftedness, appearance, or deep knowledge. It's about being faithful to serve—available to God and willing to learn right where we are. David, who would become the king of Israel, did not look anything like a royal leader. But God told Samuel to anoint him anyway, for "man looks at the outward appearance, but the Lord looks at the heart" (1 Samuel 16:7). If you are faithful, available, and teachable, then God is not concerned about the outward appearances such as worldly qualifications and qualities; He is looking at your heart.

God is working in you. If you are being called to a life of discipleship, you'll need to take a step of faith. Out of compassion and sympathy for others, you will take the initiative to reach out, provide a place for friendship, and seek to be the hands, heart, and words of God to those near you who long for this. That's when you move from being a passive bystander to being a life-giver. That's when you say, "Because it is what God desires, I want to serve others to please His heart, out of love for Him. I will be a reflection of His words, His hands of help, His compassion in my world."

It's said that success proceeds first from showing up, but it goes a step further for believers. Flourishing in community often comes from just getting together. The exhortation in Hebrews to "encourage one another" requires a group of more than one Christian. When you bring others together, you are creating the opportunity for the Spirit to show up, to blow through your gathering. It won't happen unless someone initiates. You don't have to have it all together to bring others into your space. Just do it.

Women will come to your table feeling defeated, depressed, and without hope. Life can be hard, and hope can be fleeting. But you have the opportunity to speak of God's love, faithfulness, and mercy to the women who enter your home—to remind them that our hope is in Christ and in the faithfulness of God. That word of hope must come from a heart that has recalled to mind—every morning!—the blessings and provisions of God. The grace and truth you bring to the hearts around your table will inspire them, in turn, with the hope they need to be faithful.

As you engage in teatime discipleship, your role is about so much more than facilitating fellowship. It is also about preserving and passing on God's truth. The same conviction that leads you to embrace the reality of Jesus should drive you to take your role as His disciple seriously. It's the same conviction that drove the apostles as they started the church after Jesus left them. It's the same conviction, driven by the same scriptures, that continues to grow the church today. The biblical methods for expressing those convictions have remained the same since Jesus gave us our marching orders as His disciples.

Some women are ready and eager to extend the hospitality of God to reach others. Others are cautiously confident, willing to consider giving it a go. And others are emotionally resistant, thinking they are neither qualified nor gifted to actually teach. Whichever woman you are, here's a truth for you: Discipleship is not just about what you think you can or should do for God, but about what God says He can and will do through you when you are a willing tool in His hands.

And remember, becoming a faithful disciple who ministers to others does not happen overnight. Over time, the more you step out in faith and minister to others, teaching them as you have been taught, the more you will "grow up in all aspects into Him who is the head, that is, Christ" (Ephesians 4:15). You will be blessed because of your faith, and women all around will be blessed through you.

◆

In our homes, the center of our ministry, people will watch us pour out our lives and be caught up in the beauty of kindness, captured by the beauty that reflects Christ in our moments.

THE HEART OF A DISCIPLE

A woman who follows Christ...

...seeks to know Him, holding fast to His teaching and
constantly learning more of His ways.

...notices His fingerprints in everyday life—a sunset, a frolicking puppy dog, a
fully bloomed rose—captivated by the beauty that reflects God's artistry.

...practices the habit of thankfulness, noticing Him in the moments of life, and
offers her praise and heartfelt gratitude to God in worship.

...is faithful to serve, willing to learn, and available to God's impressing her heart.

...seeks to captivate hearts with a passion for Christ, teaching
others to focus on Him on the journey ahead.

...influences others in all moments of her life. She isn't just passing on a message,
but is offering God's relationship, love, and beauty through her own life. The more
she practices these rhythms, the more they take root in her heart and responses.

Discipleship is not just about what you think you can or should do for God, but
about what God says He can and will do through you. If you are a woman of God
who is faithful and available, He can and will use you.

A LIFE-GIVING LEGACY

You may encounter many defeats, but you must not be defeated. In fact, it may be necessary to encounter the defeats, so you can know who you are, what you can rise from, how you can still come out of it.

MAYA ANGELOU

Every year, nearly five million people—some twenty thousand each day during the summer holidays—travel to the Vatican to view a legendary artistic wonder: the ceiling of the Sistine Chapel. Inaugurated just 20 years after Columbus's voyage to America, the incredible frescoes cause viewers to crane their necks and then draw in their breath as they share Michelangelo's vision.

But painting the Sistine Chapel's ceiling had never been the vision Michelangelo had for his life. He considered himself a sculptor, the crafter of the similarly legendary *Pietà* and *David*. (If you can ever glimpse even a photo of the *Pietà*, do so! It's such a beautiful rendering of Mary and her precious child, Jesus.)

Because he considered himself primarily a sculptor, Michelangelo took the work on begrudgingly, but he quickly gained a vision of his own for the ceiling. The original design had been for a painting of Jesus and the 12 disciples, but Michelangelo expanded on the plans, depicting multiple Bible stories and over 300 figures.

Michelangelo had to design a new type of scaffolding to complete his work: a wooden platform held up by brackets inserted into holes in the wall of the chapel. He worked on the painting in stages, requiring the scaffolding to be moved from one area to another. As a sculptor, he wanted his painting to have depth, and he used the common fresco technique wherein washes of paint were applied to wet plaster. He carved the plaster before painting in order to create visible outlines around the figures, an effect singular to his work. It was a backbreaking, messy, complicated endeavor.

The creation of this remarkable artifact was full of setbacks. At one stage, a fungal growth overtook the damp plaster, ruining much of what had been done. Michelangelo wrote to the pope, declaring his work to be destroyed and insisting once again that he was not a painter. The pope was not to be dissuaded, however, so Michelangelo scraped away the ruined work and began again.

His discomfort in the four years of grueling effort was such that he wrote a poem about it, lamenting his squashed stomach and face dribbled with paint from the brush held overhead all day. The poem ended with the declaration, "I am not a painter." The ceiling would take four years to complete with all its starts and stutters.

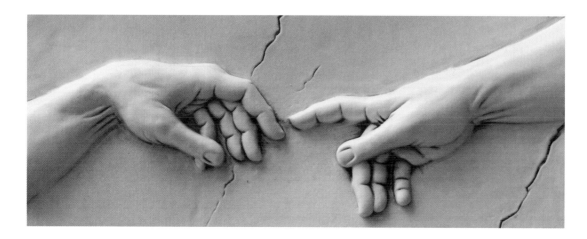

Like Michelangelo's task of crafting something beautiful, life is a long, complicated, difficult story for most of us. But when we add up a life of faithfulness—years of serving God and accumulating maturity, grace, knowledge, wisdom, and forgiveness—we will see that those years and that life have been made of thousands of moments where we chose to practice greatness, one situation at a time. Our story becomes a masterpiece, one small stroke at a time.

God has given us this opportunity, today, to invest our lives for His glory. But greatness requires endurance and perseverance. What does God require of us to accomplish His work? A steadfast heart, mind, and work ethic. A determination to keep going, keep seeking, keep trusting, keep moving ahead by faith.

> *When we go to see Jesus face-to-face, the worth of what we have accomplished will not consist of one good deed or one act of faith. It will be measured, instead, by years of practicing faithfulness, growing love, and building compassion.*

I often meet with women who want to share what is on their hearts, and I walk away amazed at the loads so many people bear. Too many of my beloved friends have a continuous stream of trials and difficulties in their lives. And even within my own family, my husband and children deal with persistent health issues, financial issues, relationship heartbreaks, and other concerns that demand decisions and attention. Whether it's a car problem, insurance paperwork, or a problem one of our children is facing as they move into their own independent lives, something will always get in the way of what we'd planned or hoped. Some of these areas of our lives have been challenging for many years without a break, and

in some cases, years of prayers have yet to be answered. Yet as I strained toward making sense of these difficult years, I found that I cultivated a more authentic compassion for other's burdens, failures, and disappointments.

Burdens are part of living in a fallen world. But we don't need to let those burdens crush us. They can help us become conformed to the likeness of our gentle, generous, loving God.

Sympathy, compassion, and humility have come to me over a lifetime, and the suffering that brought them has suited me more for ministry. In walking hand in hand with Christ through my trials, I have grown in my ability to serve others more authentically. Your story becomes your platform for serving others with love and understanding.

In Romans 8:28, the apostle Paul writes, "God causes all things to work together for good to those who love God, to those who are called according to His purpose." And why? The next verse tells us He is conforming us—shaping us—to the image of His Son, Jesus.

I am learning to see God's shadow behind all that is in my life. He has used every situation so faithfully over the years, just as He promises. As we practice patience, endurance, and perseverance, may we become faithful images, clear representations of our faithful God.

———————————————— ◆ ————————————————

God clearly doesn't have the short-term, just-getting-everything-we-want in mind. He desires to build and shape our character, knowing our ultimate happiness is dependent on our ability to love the things that are eternal and really satisfy. He is teaching us not to depend on the temporary things that keep us from putting our trust and hope in Him.

In fact, James 1:2 tells us to "consider it all joy" when we meet various trials. Most of us find this wonderful advice to be wonderfully difficult! It's interesting to me that the phrase "consider it" here can also be translated *lead, rule,* or *command.* Following this teaching will mean taking charge of our emotions and responses to the difficulties we encounter.

Joy is a big word, full of exuberance and noise and possibly confetti cannons—not a word we use very often anymore, and certainly not a word we use in relationship to trials. The funny thing is, the other scriptural usages of this term—*chara* in the Greek—include the shepherds' reaction to the star announcing Jesus's birth, the man's reaction to finding a pearl of great price, and the disciples' reaction to finding Jesus's tomb empty. Those are some confetti-cannon events in my book!

Sweet friend, do not lose heart. Your troubles are real, but in Paul's words, they are "producing for us an eternal weight of glory far beyond all comparison" (2 Corinthians 4:17). We cannot see the renewal with our eyes; at times, all we can see is the constant wearing away. But we are invited to fix our eyes on that yet-unseen glory that awaits all who live and hope in Christ.

We exult in the hope of God's glory. That's the easy part. It's the next part that's a challenge: "Not only this, but we also celebrate in our tribulations" (Romans 5:3). The word translated *celebrate* here is also translated as *glory* and sometimes *boast*. Stop and think about that for a moment: Paul instructs us to glory in, to boast about, the oppression, affliction, and distress we experience. There's a reason for this, of course. He goes on to say that tribulation brings about perseverance, perseverance brings about proven character, proven character brings about hope...and hope does not disappoint.

Life is a long story. The sum of what we have accomplished when we go to see Jesus face to face will not be measured by one deed or one act of faith. It will be measured by years of growing love, stretching compassion, persevering under trials, and practicing faith in the darkness—over and over. When we add up a life of faithfulness in serving God, accumulating maturity, grace, knowledge, wisdom, failure, forgiveness, and compassion along the way, we will see thousands of moments of choosing to persevere, one moment at a time.

But it is only in making those small choices, when no one else can see them, that we find ourselves progressing on the path of the righteous. Leaving a legacy of faith requires a lifetime of living steadfastly through each season and its demands.

As you contemplate Him and His work, may you decide to keep fervent, patient, and strong in His call to work through you. May your life bring His kingdom work to bear on a world that is desperate for His touch, light, love, and redemption.

CONVERSATION AND CONTEMPLATION

What are your eyes currently set on? What might you do today to help your focus shift from the situation immediately surrounding you to the eternal, unseen glory that is being worked out through those situations?

Does hope come naturally to you, or do you struggle to remain hopeful in dark times? How might having developed a "proven character" bring about hope in one's life?

CHOOSING PEACE

It is far better to light the candle than to curse the darkness.

WILLIAM L. WATKINSON

As a young missionary in Communist countries many years ago, I cut my teeth on discipleship—"making disciples of all nations," learning to live by faith in a very foreign place, and holding fast to my Bible. One of my surprises, however, was the prevalence of conflict and issues, at times among the missionaries themselves.

Young and unseasoned, I believed that if someone was brave and courageous enough to go into the mission field, they would probably be superhuman and surely super-spiritual! And yet, living overseas can be so very stressful that it magnifies difficulties. This was the place I began to learn the importance of peacemaking, when disharmony infiltrated the relationships on my staff team. Most were mature believers, but each needed the mercy and grace of God and from me. (Kind of reminds me of marriage!) Discord of large proportions could disrupt our unity, causing multiple issues.

Fighting, warring, and arguing are some of the foundational evidences that this world is separated from God. We war against each other as countries but also as individuals because we are self-centered. We are focused on our own agenda and our own well-being as opposed to focusing on serving and bringing harmony to others. As believers, we should not be surprised by relational conflict; it is a mark of the fallen world. And we, as followers of Christ, are called to redeem broken places.

Becoming a peacemaker in this world is an act of will, an obedience of conscience where we serve God by doing what is right. Maturity in Christ is learning to do what is right because righteousness is deeply instilled in the pathways of our minds and hearts. If we have memorized God's Word and wisdom principles, when we later encounter animosity—and we surely will, daily!—our minds will already have a plan so we can behave as Christ would have us behave. Truth, understanding, and obedience are partners in peacemaking.

Peace I leave you, My peace I give you.

JOHN 14:27

Jesus said, "Blessed are the peacemakers, for they will be called sons of God" (Matthew 5:9). What a defining verse! By becoming peacemakers, we will be observed to be God's children, working to make His kingdom a reality here on earth. But the verse also implies that peace does not come easily. This is the work of a lifetime—something that must be created.

Every relationship, by default, is between two selfish, sinful people. The question in relationship struggles is not who is right, but who will make peace, give grace, and forgive. Making peace starts inside, with a decision that says, "If I am willing to humble myself and reach out, I can become a vehicle to bring peace and restoration to this relationship." We can be vessels for God to show His love to the people around us. We don't shirk the cost of making peace with others—the cost of bowing our own hearts to our pride and becoming willing to serve the one with whom we have conflict.

Whether as spouses, parents, friends, siblings, or coworkers, peacemaking—the act of choosing to reach out in the work of restoration—comes from a heart that worships God. Humbling ourselves brings the possibility of unity and restoration as we admit the ways we fail and disappoint people who trusted us. By our own kindness, we can show the world that humility is the bridge to making peace.

James 3:17 teaches, "The wisdom from above is first pure, then peace-loving, gentle, reasonable, full of mercy and good fruits, impartial, free of hypocrisy." May the Holy Spirit quicken our hearts to obey and practice this truth, that we might bridge the gaps in our relationships with the love of God.

Are there any relationships God is pressing on your heart to restore? Is anything keeping you from making peace with those who are in conflict with you? Do you need to humble yourself or forgive the other person? If I have learned anything from the heart of Jesus, it is that when I choose to obey what He shows me in His Word, that obedience ultimately brings me peace and deep joy. I do not have to carry hate or bitterness; He will relieve me from them when I accept His will for me to make peace.

Peacemaking— the act of choosing to reach out in the work of restoration—comes from a heart that worships God.

A memory that is burned into my soul was the last phrase someone I loved said about me before she died. Dementia had overwhelmed her brain, and often, a mean-spirited vocabulary seeped from her lips. Her last words to me were negative, hurtful, and petty, and they have created shadows over my heart many times. A legacy of hatefulness is not reflective of Christ through us.

Several verses have become my foundation for understanding the context of others, for seeking to avoid unnecessary conflict.

"A gentle answer turns away wrath" (Proverbs 15:1). Speaking gently to one I am tempted to injure with my words has calmed many the relational storm.

"Love covers a multitude of sins" (1 Peter 4:8) and *"Love...is the perfect bond of unity" (Colossians 3:14).* Pondering these verses has led me to the wisdom of choosing love when anger was close by.

Jesus became my model of a different way of leaving a legacy. He gave His life for my benefit—freely, generously. As He chose to serve me, us, I have understood that service is what I must pursue as well. It is natural to be self-absorbed, supernatural to serve others. And in choosing to be a servant, I know I cannot frivolously throw words around that might cause hurt or a sense of failure in the lives of others. And so, I have learned little by little to give love and forgiveness, serving because I know it to be the only way to heal and be restored. He alone showed me how.

◆

Speak these words of peacemaking:
I'm sorry.
I was wrong.
I forgive you.
I love you.
I understand.
And remember that today, God offers His peace to you.

IN THIS TIME AND PLACE

Someone is sitting in the shade today because
someone planted a tree a long time ago.

WARREN BUFFETT

Standing at my front door, I looked out at an ocean of cars parked in every conceivable spot in our wide driveway (I counted 20 there!). Down the street and around the corner was an endless line of cars parked tightly in every space on our short cul-de-sac. Amazement and grace filled my heart.

God is so good, and He sends grace when we ask Him to work in our lives. Many years ago, after yet another move, I was feeling lonely and unsupported in my stage of life. I knew I needed fellowship, but I didn't know of a group or Bible study where I would find like-minded friends. If I wanted a group, I would have to start it!

So I put out an announcement to all the people I knew from various activities I was beginning to commit to. I invited moms in for Bible study, snacks, and fellowship at my home once a month. In the first year or so, my little group grew to fill the room. We would begin in the early evening, making introductions so no strangers felt left out. Women took turns bringing delectable snacks. After a half hour of chatting and sharing with friends, I opened

my Bible or a book we were reading together. At the end of the evening, we prayed for many requests that came from the group. And then more conversation bubbled about in every corner. Sometimes I would say goodnight and go upstairs to bed at 11:00 p.m., and still the women would stay and talk with one another! My goal was to leave each one with the mercy, tenderness, and the unconditional love of Christ, as I knew most moms feel incompetent amid their myriad life demands.

I loved having these women in my home, but eventually our group ran out of room. We had 90 people coming regularly, perching wherever they could find space in my living room, dining room, and entrance hall. People finally started sitting all the way up our front stairway!

One evening, our group swelled to 180. Midway through the event, the doorbell rang. A police officer was standing at the door, and he told us in no uncertain terms that we had a parking problem. Too many cars were parked in our residential area; we'd grown too big for our neighborhood's britches. Clay and I approached our church for help, asking if we could hold our Bible study in their fellowship hall. They agreed to host our tribe, and when we held our first meeting, 260 women showed up!

Clay and I had no special ability, no strategic angle to grow a ministry. We were simply available. When God called, we said yes. That remains our commitment today—saying yes, whether that means hosting ten women or a hundred.

Jesus's simple command to "make disciples," carried forward by His Spirit-empowered followers, has fueled and fired the growth of Christianity for 2,000 years, and it will continue to do so until the end of the age. You are a part of that wildfire of faith. You're adding fuel to that fire when you respond to the Great

Commission of Jesus by going to your world—your neighborhood, your church, your community, your city—to make disciples. Just like the apostles who spread Christ's teaching of the kingdom of God in *their* place and time, you are empowered by the Spirit of Christ within you to be a witness and worker for Jesus in *your* place and time. You "go" because Jesus is with you, *in* you, empowering you by the Holy Spirit to be His witness in your little corner of the "remotest part of earth." No matter who you are, God wants to use you to make disciples.

All ministry in Christ's name—in every place to every person of every time—begins with Jesus's final words that conclude Matthew's Gospel:

I heard the voice of the Lord, saying, "Whom shall I send, and who will go for Us?" Then I said, "Here am I. Send me!"
ISAIAH 6:8

All authority in heaven and on earth has been given to Me.
Go, therefore, and make disciples of all the nations, baptizing
them in the name of the Father and the Son and the Holy Spirit,
teaching them to follow all that I commanded you; and behold, I
am with you always, to the end of the age.

MATTHEW 28:18-20

For 40 days after His resurrection, Jesus appeared to His followers and instructed His apostles about the kingdom of God. At the end of that time, He gathered the apostles together, promising them that they would "receive power" when the Holy Spirit came upon them and that they would become His witnesses—not just in Israel, but to all the earth (Acts 1:8). Now you, too, are invited to be a witness!

How does Christ's last command to "make disciples" apply to you, right here and right now? How can you be a disciple of Christ, ready to make disciples?

Where and when can you "go" and make disciples? Are you standing still, or are you moving forward for Jesus and His kingdom? What part of the world can you reach?

PART FOUR

SACRED DAYS

I buy most of my teacups secondhand. If you were to stand at my cupboard and look at the cups, you'd see that none of them match—I've found them at different times and places. Many of them have stains, cracks, and signs of long use. To me, these cracks and stains are part of the teacups' stories, and the stories of the people who used them long before they came to my home.

There's nothing new about my teapots either. I like to roam the small shops and stalls in Oxford, seeking out older silver teapots. When I find them, they're a bit battered and bruised, often darkened with age and rust. I barter for them, getting them cheap, and then I bring them home and get out the polish. These old silver teapots hold the heat far longer than ceramic pots, letting you linger at the table before the tea goes cold.

I love to collect these old items—the ones of little worth to many people, perhaps. And when friends old and new come to my home, I open the cupboard and ask them to choose a cup. They'll select a cup that's just right for them, and then we'll linger at the table, adding a new conversation to that cup's history.

Cultivating a life filled with beautiful rhythms, life-giving rituals, and attitudes of gratefulness shapes our hearts and minds amid the storms. Our agency to believe in God's goodness and faithfulness will make every day meaningful, every day a gift, as we wait with hope.

BECOMING HOME TO ONE ANOTHER

We carry our homes within us, which enables us to fly.

JOHN CAGE

Have you ever moved away from a home where you've lived a long time—perhaps a home you didn't want to leave? And at first, when you got to your new home, all you could think about was what you missed, not what you had that was new and full of possibility. Until you met a new friend who reminded you that it would get better—someone who encouraged and loved you. You were far from home and felt all alone, but that friend, and others you made along the way, helped you through the changes and upheaval you faced.

As I've moved over and over again, *home* has been what I carried in my heart. I have been able to welcome others into my space because the beauty of home rested there. Creating legacies of beauty and hospitality was not dependent on the walls, grounds, or furniture, but on our hearts, traditions, and feasting. Wherever we've lived, comfort has been given.

The biblical book of Hebrews was written to Jewish

believers who had been scattered by the persecution in Jerusalem after the stoning of Stephen. They left behind the temple, sacrifices, and traditions—the familiar sights, sounds, and smells of the holy city that had made their faith a tangible experience. Now, they were being asked to live by the intangible beliefs of their new Christian faith, by the Holy Spirit within them. It was hard to believe in Jesus, and some wanted to return to the familiar security of "home" in Jerusalem. But the book's writer reminds the believers what they need to do when they're alone and far from the familiar: to be faithful and to encourage one another.

> *Let's hold firmly to the confession of our hope without wavering, for He who promised is faithful; and let's consider how to encourage one another in love and good deeds, not abandoning our own meeting together, as is the habit of some people, but encouraging one another; and all the more as you see the day drawing near.*

HEBREWS 10:23-25

Just like those early Christians, we, too, are far from home. Only the Word of God and the fellowship of other believers enable us to "hold firmly to the confession of our hope without wavering" (verse 23). It's a long journey between here and heaven, but God is with us and is faithful to keep His promises.

The life of faith is not always easy. Life can become difficult, and we can lose our confidence in Christ. That is why we need one another; endurance is not meant to be a solo effort.

CONVERSATION AND CONTEMPLATION

How can you "hold firmly to the confession" of all that you hope for in Christ? What can cause that hope to waver? What promises of God strengthen your faith and steady your hope?

May God give you strength for each day and the vision to know that even in the small details of your life, the kingdom of righteousness is growing. May your home manifest His grace!

SHINING IN THE DARKNESS

*The power of finding beauty in the humblest
things makes home happy and life lovely.*

LOUISA MAY ALCOTT, *Jack and Jill*

The last guest opened the front door. Crystal candles atop a crimson tablecloth flickered and sparkled on the Victorian china from a great-grandmother's dowry. Bedecked in frilly dresses, rouged cheeks, and lipsticked mouths, 14 mothers and daughters bashfully took their chairs around our dining room table.

The event marked our first ever traditional mother-daughter Christmas tea. My hopes were that as Sarah's friends and their mothers met together, we could share intimate thoughts, hear of the girls' dreams, and build a foundation of friendship. Since then, our Christmas tea has become an annual event—a marker in our calendars to come together and celebrate our friendship and our Savior. Thirty years of teas have made for endearing memories.

These teas have taken on different forms over the years, as we've moved from place to place and celebrated in different settings. One recent year, when we couldn't gather indoors due to COVID-19 restrictions, we set up folding chairs and a couple of small tables outside our front door, loading trays with cinnamon buns and mugs of hot

cocoa for a chilly gathering! But some elements are constant: We tell stories, we feast on good food, and we always invite a stranger. We welcome someone into our circle who could use the healing power of fellowship, community, and love.

More than the gifts, more than the sparkle, more than the array of cups and saucers, God's love for us in Christ is what I seek to share during Christmas. Long after each year's festivities have been forgotten, our dear ones will remember the happiness shared together. That's a gift that will remain with them their whole lives long! If we have a heart that says, "I receive you into my life as a gift from God," if we intentionally provide words of life and encouragement, they will come to us again and again for the Spirit they need to feel, hear, and be comforted by in every season.

> *Do not neglect hospitality to strangers, for by this some have entertained angels without knowing it.*
> **HEBREWS 13:2**

The world around us holds temptation and darkness. That is why we all long for a place of comfort, a sanctuary in which to restore the light in our souls, and where we can experience the truth of God's love for us—through all our senses! When a child sits under a sparkling Christmas tree and hears that it was God who said, *"Light shall shine out of darkness" (2 Corinthians 4:6),* she understands God as a light who brightens. *"Taste and see that the Lord is good" (Psalm 34:8)* is much more easily imagined in a home where hot cinnamon rolls are eaten together just as soon as they emerge from the oven. And *"Glory to God in the highest, and on earth peace among people with whom He is pleased" (Luke 2:14)* is envisioned in a home where the sparkles of beauty reflect a heavenly sky and voices are raised in songs of praise.

The rhythms of tradition, of coming together in celebration year in and year out, show us that we belong to one another, and that we belong to God. Whatever tradition you cultivate in your home and community, let it be one that puts a stamp of remembrance on your heart, and one that ties family and friends close together.

I have lived in tiny apartments and
sprawling old houses, and I have found that beauty
expressed through your own design is what makes a home.
Sometimes a little candlelight in a cozy room is all you need to
create a place of rest and a sense of heaven.

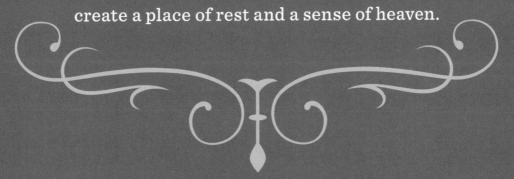

TEATIME

If you'd like to start your own Christmas tea tradition, here's everything you need to get started. Of course, you can supplement this menu with your favorite holiday treats—perhaps a few types of Christmas candies or warming cups of mulled apple cider. You might even invite each guest to bring a dozen of her favorite holiday cookies for an exchange.

Chilled raspberry soup

Curried chicken salad with pecans, grapes, and vanilla yogurt

Mixed greens with feta, cranberries, and toasted nuts

Chocolate chip mousse cake

Yorkshire Gold tea in one pot and decaf spiced tea (your choice) in the other

I first had this delicious soup one hot summer when I was traveling in Budapest, Hungary. Because it's chilled, it's so very refreshing! We serve it every year at the start of our Christmas tea, pouring it into pedestal crystal sundae dishes and topping it with a dollop of whipped cream.

A Christmas Tea

Chilled Raspberry Soup

18-20 ounces raspberries
*(I buy frozen berries and thaw them
in my fridge the day before I make
the soup)*

1 1/2 cups water

**1 1/4 cups cranberry-apple
juice** *or* **cranberry-
raspberry juice**

3/4 cup sugar

2 tsp ground cinnamon

1/4 tsp ground cloves

2 Tbsp lemon juice

8 ounces raspberry yogurt

Whipped cream for serving

In a blender, puree raspberries and water. You can strain out the seeds to make it totally smooth if you like. Transfer puree to a large saucepan and stir in the cranberry juice, sugar, cinnamon, and cloves. Taste the mixture: If your berries are on the sour side, you might need a little more sugar. Bring to a boil over medium heat.

Once the mixture has come to a boil, remove from heat and let sit. Once cool, whisk in lemon juice and yogurt. Refrigerate until ready to serve.

Pour into small bowls and top with a dollop of whipped cream.

Curried Chicken Salad *with Pecans, Grapes, and Vanilla Yogurt*

**Meat pulled and shredded
from a rotisserie chicken**

1/2 cup mayonnaise

1/2 cup vanilla yogurt

1 Tbsp honey or raw sugar

2 tsp curry powder

3/4 cup toasted pecans

1/2 cup green onion, minced

**1 1/2 cups sliced grapes
(purple or green—or both!)**

**1/2 cup sweetened dried
cranberries**

Salt and pepper to taste

Mix mayonnaise, yogurt, and honey together with the curry powder. Set aside.

In a large bowl, combine shredded chicken, pecans, green onion, grapes, and cranberries. Pour yogurt mixture on top and toss well to combine.

Mixed Greens with Feta, Cranberries, and Toasted Nuts

2 heads romaine *or* **2 bags of mixed baby greens**
1/2 cup chopped green onions
3/4 cup crumbled feta
3/4 cup chopped salted walnuts *or* **chopped roasted butter pecans**
3/4 cup sweetened dried cranberries

I love to make salads that are full of texture, color, and taste. This makes a perfect Christmas salad with the red and green accents.

Wash and dry your greens and place in large salad bowl. Toss with green onions, feta, nuts, and cranberries. Serve with your favorite salad dressing.

Chocolate Chip Mousse Cake

1 large package instant chocolate pudding
1 extra egg above what the cake mix calls for
1/2 cup extra water
1 cup chocolate chips

This is what I call my cheat cake. It has been a favorite for many years. It's such a rich treat and looks beautiful on a cake pedestal.

Buy a fudge or chocolate boxed cake mix. Follow the directions but add the ingredients on the left.

Bake according to directions on the box. I usually put this in a Bundt pan, and it feeds more people that way. After you remove the cake from the pan, fill a tea strainer with powdered sugar and sprinkle atop the cake. You can also use chocolate frosting if you prefer.

THE CUP WE'RE GIVEN

*Surely every body is aware of the divine pleasures which attend a
winter fire-side: candles at four o'clock, warm hearth-rugs, tea, a
fair tea-maker, shutters closed, curtains flowing in ample draperies
on the floor, whilst the wind and rain are raging audibly without.*

THOMAS DE QUINCEY

I am independent by nature. I am used to working hard
to take care of life's many details on my own. I walk five
miles a day and do not slow down for anything or anyone.
But recently, my doctor proclaimed that I had worn out all
the cartilage supporting my hip and that I would need a hip
replacement. I found myself experiencing eye-watering
pain; I could barely take a few steps without stopping to
take a deep breath. On top of this, a bulging disc in my back
was wreaking further havoc. The slightest movement was
painful.

I hate to be vulnerable and place a burden on people—yet
there I was, humbled by a newfound need to rely on others.
I had no choice but to wait until someone brought me a cup
of tea instead of going down my steep steps to the kitchen
one more time. Clay and I didn't have a car at our home in
England, so I had to order taxis instead of walking places
with my family. And I needed help shopping for groceries,
as usually I do it on foot.

I was struggling with the "cup of life" I'd been given at this moment in time. This part of my story would require some adjustment.

In Scripture, a cup can function as a metaphor for "portion." David, then, could speak of his cup overflowing in the experience of God's goodness, and Jesus could ask that the Father would let the cup of suffering pass from Him. I was certainly ready for my own suffering to pass! But the Lord had something different in mind.

Every once in a while, God shows His very personal kindness in generous, considerate ways that we would never have known to ask for. For three weeks after surgery, friends brought me meals. Flowers flourished on tables throughout my living room where I spent my days on the couch. Each morning, my wonderful husband, Clay, would shoulder me down the steep stairs, stoop over and put my socks on my cold toes, and steep me a perfect cup of tea, with just the right amount of sugar and milk. Setting the books and trinkets and things I needed on a table next to me, he spoiled me with attention to details—his strength. I don't remember feeling so loved and cared for in my whole life. I was usually the one pouring out my life. Now, this thoughtfulness touched deep places in my heart I didn't know I needed.

For the first time in many years, I found myself with an abundance of time on my hands. Realizing anew that friendships grow strongest when personal time is invested, I used that time for deep conversations with those I loved.

Our defense against hard times is honest and heartfelt fellowship accompanied by steaming cups of tea and something wonderful to eat.

As I grow older, I am learning how much kindness means to me—what a blessing it is to be served so sweetly. A person giving out of the overflow of her own life is a picture of Christ Himself. It is the kindness of God I have experienced, and now I am more than ever moved to become more actively kind and considerate to others who need my attention.

Perhaps you are looking at the "cup" of your life, seeing all its chips and cracks, and wishing you'd been given another. I certainly would have traded mine at times, given the chance! And in doing

so, I would have missed out on God's blessing through the sacrificial kindness of others. Their actions sanctified—made holy—the experience of my suffering.

Holiness requires that we choose to believe in God's presence, purpose, and attention in every moment, every day. We believe in the dark times of life. We worship and sing to Him when we want to hide under the covers. We wait as long as it takes to see His answer to our prayers—and we're so often surprised by the answer. We wait on God and God alone.

We want to be faithful until we see Him face-to-face. All of life, it seems, works against our faithfulness. Both spiritually and physically, we are weak and vulnerable. We are surrounded by the voices of the world and tempted regularly. But in all of it, God is cheering us on, hoping we will stand fast, desiring our hearts to remain holy and faithful to Him.

PRAYER

DEAREST JESUS,

Help me to see the cup of life you have given me as a place I might worship You. "Not my will but Yours be done." When I learn to see the beauty of Your presence in every moment, to accept my limitations, and to live into Your grace, I understand more Your generous, humble life that cost You everything. Let me minister to others from the warm and healing grace You have given me, from the humility of understanding my limitations, that I might have compassion and sympathy for all You bring my way. It is not in controlling life but in submitting to Your ways with joy that I can encourage the hearts of others.

AMEN.

TO LOVE AND LAY
DOWN YOUR LIFE

When you pour yourself out upon us, you do not sink
to the lowest level, but you raise us up; you are not
dispersed, but rather you gather us together.

AUGUSTINE

Recently, a writing deadline was upon me. A speaking engagement (and not one in my wheelhouse) loomed. Four different houseguests were coming in the next week, and my local Bible study of 20 women was due to meet in my home that night. I woke up that day already feeling tired from all the responsibilities ahead.

One of my adult children called. Lingering on the phone with me a bit too long signaled to me there were some unspoken issues. The Holy Spirit seemed to nudge my heart and say, "This is a strategic moment—use it well."

"Would you like to meet me for a late breakfast in a few minutes? Let's celebrate this day together, and then we can move on to our responsibilities," I said. So we met. As it ends up, this sweet one had huge issues to share with me— burdens, fears, weariness. Yet our time together brought a smile back to my loved one, a sense of hope for the days ahead.

So many times, I have had to move my expectations and commitments aside to have a divine appointment with someone right in front of me. Each day, the Spirit stands at the doorways of our homes to compel us to enter and remain in a place of life, comfort, rest, beauty. Some days we are ready to receive, and we gladly submit our schedules and energy to His will. But sometimes we say, "My life is already so busy; I don't have time to add one more ideal."

The dilemma, then, is how to weave beauty, color, and celebration into an already busy life. Understanding *why* we take the trouble to bring His Spirit's presence into the moments of our lives gives emotional and spiritual fuel to keep going through the years. Honoring Jesus's sacrificial love by surrendering the moments

of our lives to Him allows us to follow in His footsteps and gain a more personal knowledge of what He did for us. We may not be facing hungry lions in the Colosseum, but we're still laying down our lives for His sake—day in, day out. In John 15:13, Jesus told us, "Greater love has no one than this, that a person will lay down his life for his friends." You, too, can lay down your time, your heart, and your everyday moments for the people within your orbit.

Jesus—knowing that He had cast the stars into their place, that He existed for eternity past in a splendor of light and in perfect fellowship with the Father, where myriads of angels bowed before Him and worshiped—girded Himself with a towel, knelt down, and wiped the dust from His beloved friends' dirty feet. All of this for those who could not have known the sacrifice that was coming, the depth of His choice to humble Himself, or the vast generosity that was being expended from a heart overflowing with love focused on them. Only maturity would bring gratitude.

And so, in pondering, I must ask myself: *Does my heart remain humble as I wash feet or serve a meal? Are my words life-giving and generous, serving to strengthen those in my home or nearby with my heart, like the heart of Jesus? Do I bow willingly in the dust of my own life because He was so willing to spend His life in giving, serving, and loving without thought of Himself, even in His death?*

In our everyday circumstances, most of our work is invisible. This noble cause we embrace is often fraught with challenges, exhaustion, and relentless repetition. Yet this is the very place of our worship. This is the place faith is being forged and character is being modeled and love is going deep into the hearts and minds of those we impact. What you are doing matters so much. And most of all, Jesus—who sacrificed His time, His emotions, and ultimately His body and freedom—sees you and is so very pleased. I've been surprised by how this season of life—my sixties—has been deeply satisfying. The giving up of myself reaped satisfying fruit in close relationships with my family and friends.

 *We are a picture of God's sacrificial love to the minds, souls, and hearts of those He entrusts into our hands.*

A DELIGHTFUL
DISCIPLESHIP

The cup of tea on arrival at a country house is a thing which, as a rule,
I particularly enjoy. I like the crackling logs, the shaded lights, the
scent of buttered toast, the general atmosphere of leisured coziness.

P.G. WODEHOUSE, *The Code of the Woosters*

"Why do you think you and your siblings all love the Lord as adults?"

Sarah looked at me thoughtfully and then answered, "I think it was the French toast, buttered pecans, and maple syrup!"

This has become an oft-repeated story in our family because it reflects our family culture and discipleship philosophy. For our children to learn to love God, they must see our love for God in the way we sing around the house, the way we sip a cool drink on the porch while enjoying the summer flowers, and at the "Kiss me goodnight?" bedtime moments.

Sometimes I think Christians feel guilty about enjoying life too much, as though God is more pleased with service, seriousness, or a somber expression. Yet God intended that we as adults enjoy our days and find satisfaction in them. As we walk hand in hand with God, we are intended to experience pleasure and fulfillment. If we see passing on faith as a mere obligation, our lives will overflow with duty and pressure, and we will become discouraged and weary. God did not make us to be slaves of works, and God didn't make us to use us—He is complete. God wanted sons and daughters to love, communicate with, and engage with. He wants to enjoy and be close to us as a parent longs to be near beloved children. He created a gorgeous world to enjoy, food to feast on, experiences to enjoy. As one of my children told me, "Mama, I'm so glad our God is the God of puppy dogs, spicy fajitas, and music to dance to."

We must perceive the proper vision of His love and commitment to us if we are to pass on a faith that will engage the people around us. Will we model a faith of resigned endurance or delighted enthusiasm?

> *Our real influence comes from the way we live out our faith.*

Discipleship becomes a dependable rhythm in our homes. It is woven into every moment of family life—when we rise up, when we sit down, whenever we are alone with our children, and when we gather together as an entire family. It is not just about passing on doctrine or theological concepts, but about relationship, love, and beauty.

Like you, I've gone through times when I can't seem to get anything together. Life demands so much of us, and every kind of catastrophe—from broken bones to broken hearts—seems to pile on all the more during the seasons when we can't manage one more thing. God wants us to find joy and peace even in these times.

We often suffer under the illusion that if we get enough massages, find the right counselor, or hire a housecleaning service, we'll have peace. But our contentment can't depend on any outside circumstances. No massage can make you strong. No counselor can move you forward. No housekeeper can give you the uncluttered spirit you long for. You have to decide that you have the capacity, the ability to keep going. One more day. One more step.

I have never perfectly lived up to my ideals. But if I've shown God's love to anyone, it's because I believed it was more important than any other aspect of my faith. We don't always have to *feel* like loving, we just need to act in a loving way. On days when I just didn't want to prepare my home to welcome women, when I felt awkward inviting a near-stranger to tell me her story, when I could hardly handle another day of children's interruptions, I remembered that the God who loved us to the end of Himself chose to put our paths together, and if I took delight in the Lord, I could also take delight in His creations. Often, I would take one more step of obedience and watch God show up beyond my expectations.

Keep falling in love with the Lord, and you'll fall more in love with the people He gave you. Whether it's in witnessing the antics of a golden retriever or laughing around plates of butter pecan French toast, celebrate the tremendous life God has given you. Celebrate the people, and let them summon you to the joy of the Lord.

CONVERSATION AND CONTEMPLATION

The apostle Paul famously described love in 1 Corinthians 13. The words are familiar—*patient, kind, believes all things, hopes all things.* Take a few moments to read the passage, maybe aloud with a friend, or perhaps in a translation you're not accustomed to. Let the beauty of these truths surprise and touch you anew.

Now, write your own description of God's love for us. What adjectives might you use to describe God's forgiveness? What images will you use to illustrate His mercy? Make this description a hymn of praise!

TEATIME

The kitchen truly is a place filled with joyful noises—the cracking of eggs, the whistling of the tea kettle, the sizzling of the skillet, and the conversations, laughter, and teasing poured out while cooking and munching together. God has entrusted us as women to create a haven filled with beauty, smells, tastes, and sounds. We can use all our senses to captivate the people we love!

Even during the busiest of mornings, followed by a day filled with items to accomplish, you can get off to a great start by making a scrumptious breakfast. Our family French toast recipe checks all those boxes!

Butter Pecan French Toast

Butter Pecan French Toast

8 eggs

1/4-1/2 cup milk or cream

1 1/2 tsp cinnamon

8 slices bread

(mine is often homemade)

1 Tbsp butter

Toppings

Powdered sugar

Warm maple syrup

Toasted pecans

Butter

Sliced strawberries or apples

Sliced almonds

1 large cup of joyful noise

(Don't go looking for this last ingredient in the grocery aisles. Find it in the laughter of those who fill your home!)

In a wide, shallow bowl, break the eggs and beat lightly. Whisk in the milk, sugar, and cinnamon.

Heat butter in your skillet and heat on medium-low. Meanwhile, dip bread slices into the egg mixture, evenly coating both sides. I like to take a fork and carefully poke tiny holes in the bread slices while they're soaking, so they'll soak up more batter. It also allows them to "breathe" a bit and get fluffy without burning.

Place the soaked bread slices in the skillet and cook until lightly browned. Flip and cook a few minutes longer until both sides are evenly brown. Serve toppings separately in bowls, and allow each loved one to decorate their own French toast.

GOD LOVES YOU
TEN THOUSAND

"I don't feel very much like Pooh today," said Pooh.
"There, there," said Piglet. "I'll bring you tea and honey until you do."

A.A. MILNE, *Winnie-the-Pooh*

As sound asleep as one can be, I was curled up in a bundle of blankets in dreamland. Suddenly, I felt a gentle push. "Queenie, you need to wake up. You need to make me tea. Come be with me!" And so—pajama-d and groggy—I slipped downstairs, hand in hand with my precious little granddaughter. As I wrote earlier, our custom was to wake with a cup of tea together, sitting as close as we could in an overstuffed chair or sitting side by side, her in her special throne, me in mine. What a deeply heart-filling time I had cherishing every moment we had together.

As an older woman, I know that the thing she needs the most—and that I still need!—is the unshakable, steadfast love that will hold her through all the storms and seasons of her life. And so I tell her I love her, over and over again in a million ways. I want the pathways of her brain to always speak to her the rest of her life that she is beloved. I remember all too well my littles as they became teens and then adults, and how they never lost the need to know they were loved by someone who would stick with them their whole lives.

"Mama, do you still love me when I make such stupid mistakes?" My sweet teenager, many years ago, was curled up on the couch in an almost fetal position, deeply regretting something she had done and condemning herself over and over again for not refraining from the foolish behavior.

"I love you if you make ten thousand mistakes. I love you because you are mine. I love you even in spite of the mistakes you will make the rest of your life. You are so precious to me, I can hardly refrain from kissing your sweet head a million times right now."

A tiny smile curled her lips. I stroked her hair and told her that God's love became more precious to me each day, because the older I got, the more I sinned, even as I long to be good. And the more I fall short, the more I experience the depth of His love and the enormity of His grace.

All of us know that deep inside we are broken. We want to be good, to practice patience, to be generous of heart...yet our petty selves accuse us of countless ways that we fail to live up to our own standards. In a thousand ways, we fall short of God's ways. But here's the truth that changes everything:

> His love is beyond measure.
> His mercy never ends.
> His forgiveness covers all the days of my life.

Just this morning, I was awakened by a sunrise outside the bedroom window. Pink and coral danced on the clouds and seemed to shout, "This day is holy, a day to celebrate, because I am here. My love and mercy are the starting points of your day. Remember Me and live in my joy." My breath caught in my throat as I whispered,

The LORD's acts of mercy indeed do not end,
For His compassions do not fail.
They are new every morning;
Great is Your faithfulness.

LAMENTATIONS 3:22-23

Every single morning when we awaken, God's mercy sees our frailty and provides a covering of grace through every moment we fall short of perfection. This profound truth is vitally important

to being able to love God fully, to live in the deep joy and freedom He wants us to experience every day.

The truths of His forgiveness written in God's Word will transform your life every day. His life exchanged for your life means you will never have to feel separated from Him again, but every day, you can curl up in His abiding love, walk in His gracious mercy, and breathe free from the burden of guilt. Our heavenly Father waits to show you His goodness because it is at the very core of His heart. He longs for you to know His unconditional love.

Perhaps all of this sounds simple—something you've heard so long that you no longer pause to linger over it. But it is my prayer that you will experience anew the might and power and beauty of this truth: that God has forgiven every flaw, every imperfection, every sin you will ever commit, and by the power of His Spirit, we can live in peace until the day we see Him face-to-face.

PRAYER

BELOVED HEAVENLY FATHER,

Please shower these precious ones with a personal and deep knowledge of Your love for them. Fill them with the light of Your hope, beauty, creativity. Send them into their worlds to bring Your light, creativity, delight, truth, and beauty. Bless and bless and bless them, I pray.

We come with deep thanksgiving for Your grace, in Jesus's name.

AMEN.

For the LORD is good;

His mercy is everlasting

And His faithfulness is to all generations.

Psalm 100

PEOPLE TO DISCIPLE

PEOPLE TO DISCIPLE

VERSES TO SHARE

VERSES TO SHARE

PRAYERS

PRAYERS

ABOUT THE AUTHOR

Sally Clarkson is a bestselling author, world-renowned speaker, and beloved mentor who has dedicated her life to supporting and inspiring countless women to live into the story God has for them to tell.

Sally hosts a weekly podcast, *At Home with Sally*, where she invites you into her home, thoughts, and life to share her candid wisdom and winsome discipleship. The podcast reaches women around the world and now has 20 million downloads.

Sally has been married to her husband, Clay, for 41 years, and together they founded and run Whole Heart Ministries, an international ministry seeking to support families in raising faithful, healthy, and loving children in an increasingly difficult culture. They have four children—Sarah, Joel, Nathan, and Joy—each exceeding in their own fields as academics, authors, actors, musicians, filmmakers, and speakers.

Sally lives between the mountains of Colorado and the rolling fields of England and can usually be found with a cup of tea in her hands.